A Pacific Community

A PACIFIC COMMUNITY

E. GOUGH WHITLAM

Published by THE AUSTRALIAN STUDIES ENDOWMENT in collaboration with COUNCIL ON EAST ASIAN STUDIES, HARVARD UNIVERSITY and distributed by THE HARVARD UNIVERSITY PRESS, Cambridge (Massachusetts) and London 1981

The Council on East Asian Studies at Harvard University publishes a mono-
graph series and, through the Fairbank Center for East Asian Research,
administers research projects designed to further scholarly understanding of
China, Japan, Korea, Vietnam, Inner Asia, and adjacent areas.

Library of Congress Cataloging in Publication Data

Whitlam, Edward Gough, 1916–
A Pacific community.
Bibliography: p.
Includes index.
1. East Asia—Economic conditions. 2. Australia
—Economic conditions—1945–   3. East Asia—
Commerce. 4. Australia—Commerce. 5. East Asia—
Politics and government. 6. Australia—Politics
and government—1945–   I. Title.
HC460.5.W47   338.99   80-27545
ISBN 0–674–65070–0

Foreword

By 1977, as Mr. Whitlam notes in his Prologue, more American trade was flowing across the Pacific than across the Atlantic. The world's most rapid economic growth is taking place in the East Asia-Western Pacific region, and the historic period of Atlantic supremacy in the nineteenth and twentieth centuries appears rapidly to be giving way to a new Pacific supremacy.

The Pacific Ocean and its perimeter include countries of widely varying political make-up—the East Asian countries, the Philippines, Indonesia, Australia, New Zealand, the new island nations, Canada, the United States, the countries of Latin America. What kind of cooperation is desirable among such diverse nations? Is cooperation possible at all? Given the global nature of world trade and cultural relations, it is not at all apparent that regional blocs can have any meaningful exclusiveness. Yet, given the growing regional cooperation in the European Economic Community and in the Association of Southeast Asian Nations, it is quite likely that Western Pacific nations may begin to look toward new opportunities for their own regional cooperation or, at a minimum, to understandings that will govern their contacts.

With the decline of United States hegemony from its peak in the first decade after World War II, the question of mutual security against outside threats will also require a higher level of cooperation among Pacific nations. As the rising economic power in the region, Japan is certain to play a key role.

Australia's role in the Pacific region is a very special one.

Australia and New Zealand are the two Western nations on the Asian side of the Pacific. Australia is bound closely to Asia through geographical location, bound closely to Europe and North America through language, culture, and its place within the British Commonwealth. Australia is endowed with raw materials and resources sought after by the industrial powers of East Asia and elsewhere. Because of this special position, it is natural that Australia should be acutely sensitive to the opportunities and problems that are generating in the Pacific Basin.

One of Australia's most articulate spokesmen is Gough Whitlam, former leader of the Australian Labor Party and former Prime Minister, an experienced lawyer, much traveled in Europe and America, a keen observer of the Western Pacific region, and a thoughtful analyst of possible future trends there.

In the spring of 1979, Harvard had the pleasure of welcoming Mr. Whitlam as one of the first Visiting Professors of Australian Studies. During his stay at the university, Mr. Whitlam delivered three public lectures on A Pacific Community. Conscious of the importance of Mr. Whitlam's views about an area of such rising importance, we encouraged him to adapt his lectures for publication. We are happy now to make them available to the public at large.

Ezra Vogel
Council on East Asian Studies
Harvard University

Contents

Abbreviations

ABC	Australian Broadcasting Commission
ACP	African, Caribbean, and Pacific developing countries covered by the Lomé Convention
ADB	Asian Development Bank
ALP	Australian Labor Party
ANZAAS	Australian and New Zealand Association for the Advancement of Science
ANZUS	Security Treaty (Australia, New Zealand, United States) [see p. 54]
APEF	Association of Iron Ore Exporting Countries (Association des pays exportateurs de minéral de fer)
ASEAN	Association of South-East Asian Nations
ASIC	Australian Standard Industry Classification
ASPAC	Asian and Pacific Council
CIPEC	Intergovernmental Council of Copper Exporting Countries (Conseil intergouvernemental des pays exportateurs de cuivre)
DAC	Development Assistance Committee of the OECD
DMC	Developing Member Country
DPRK	Democratic People's Republic of Korea (North Korea)
ECAFE	Economic Commission for Asia and the Far East (now ESCAP)
EEC	European Economic Community
EEZ	exclusive economic zone
ESCAP	Economic and Social Commission for Asia and the Pacific (formerly ECAFE)
FEER	Far Eastern Economic Review
GATT	General Agreement on Tariffs and Trade
GDP	gross domestic product
GNP	gross national product
IAC	Industries Assistance Commission
IBA	International Bauxite Association

IBRD	International Bank for Reconstruction and Development (The World Bank)
ICFTU	International Confederation of Free Trade Unions
IDA	International Development Association
IMCO	Inter-Governmental Maritime Consultative Organization
IMF	International Monetary Fund
IPC	Integrated Programme for Commodities
MITI	Ministry of International Trade and Industry (Japan) [see p. 83]
MTN	Multilateral Trade Negotiations
NARA	Nippon-Australia Relations Agreement
NATO	North Atlantic Treaty Organization
NIEO	New International Economic Order
OECD	Organization for Economic Cooperation and Development
OPEC	Organization of the Petroleum Exporting Countries
OPTAD	Organization for Pacific Trade, Aid, and Development
PBEC	Pacific Basin Economic Council
P.L.O.	Palestine Liberation Organization
PRC	People's Republic of China
ROK	Republic of Korea (South Korea)
RSV-N	Republic of South Viet Nam
SEATO	South-East Asian Collective Defense Treaty
SRVN	Socialist Republic of Viet Nam
UNCLOS III	Third United Nations Conference on the Law of the Sea
UNCTAD	United Nations Conference on Trade and Development
UNHCR	United Nations High Commissioner for Refugees
UNIDO III	United Nations Industrial Development Organization, Third General Conference

Prologue

In July 1973, the President of the United States, in a message to the Prime Minister of Australia, invited the Australian people to join in commemorating the American Revolution on its 200th anniversary. The invitation said in part: "The President and the people of the United States hope that our two countries can use the occasion to foster not only personal contacts but the widest possible range of fruitful interchange among people in the realms of both ideas and of actions."

Two years later, obviously on the Fourth of July, I announced that the Australian government had decided to endow a Chair of Australian Studies at Harvard University. Preliminary talks with Harvard, I stated, had established that the chair would be at research level and form a center for Australian studies by other American universities. I did not envisage that I would be honored by an invitation to occupy the chair nor, I confess, that I would be free to do so.

On that Glorious Fourth in 1975, I expressed the hope that the chair would form the nucleus of expanded and continuing academic studies in America of all aspects of Australia and of Australian interests in a wider context. (I stress the regional context because I appreciate that America has now become fascinated with some countries of East Asia, even to the exclusion of other parts of East Asia or the Western Pacific in which she had taken a great interest, even an excessive or unbalanced interest, over the last twenty years.)

In three lectures, presented in April 1979 by the Council on

East Asian Studies at Harvard and which form the basis of the first three chapters of this book, I used the term *Western Pacific*. I wanted my audience and Americans generally to look not only at China and the Soviet Union, but to direct comparable attention to Japan and, I hope, to all points south of Japan. I stressed aspects of growing importance in the Western Pacific—resources, trade, politics. Western Pacific resources and trade have certainly attained great significance for the people of the United States; in 1977, U.S. trade with Asian countries for the first time exceeded U.S. trade with Europe. East Asia and the Western Pacific now form the most dynamic economy in the world. But it is also important that the political problems of the area—arising both from intra-regional relationships and from contacts between individual Western Pacific countries and other parts of the world—be better understood.

Appended to the three Harvard lectures is a fourth lecture, delivered in March 1979 to an Australia-Japan Symposium in Canberra. This brief examination of the complexities in the relationship between just two of the region's nations may suggest how vast the complexities are for all the Western Pacific. In adapting these four talks for publication, I have clarified and enlarged upon certain points; wherever there were events to report that occurred subsequently, I brought the picture up to date.

Many people have helped me in preparing the lectures for delivery and publication. My particular thanks are due to David Peetz in Canberra for helping me write the text, to Maria Brook and Suzanne Sweeney in Sydney for typing the various drafts, and to the staff at the Council on East Asian Studies for preparing transcripts.

Australian National University, Canberra
February 1980

A Pacific Community

ONE

Resources of the Pacific

At the beginning of the last century, the United States was first drawn to Australian waters by the whale oil which she required as an illuminant and a lubricant. Today, Australia's mineral and energy resources are her chief claim to significance in the world. In the Western Pacific region, the trade in minerals since World War II has been dominated by the enormous volume of Australian exports to Japan. Australia is very well endowed in minerals; Japan is very poorly endowed. The prosperity of Japan and Australia has depended very greatly during the 1960s on the U.S. corporations that have financed the exploitation of Australian resources and their export to Japanese markets. Japan has to import a great number of minerals, concentrates, and metals from Australia and also from China, Indonesia, Thailand, Malaysia, the Philippines, and Papua New Guinea. Australia exports a great number of minerals—coal, iron, manganese, aluminium, heavy beach sands, nickel, copper, zinc, lead, tungsten, and tin. Australia is the world's largest bauxite producer, the second greatest source of iron ore, the third largest nickel producer, the supplier of 15 percent of the world's hard coal trade and, potentially, 20 percent of the world's uranium.

The areas of the Pacific with the vastest resources awaiting development are in China and Siberia. The eyes of the world have been looking at the development of the former at the expense of the latter. The Soviet Union has had some success in involving Japan in the development of Siberia, for example, in the Yakutsk coal and natural gas basin, but not on a grand scale. Apart from the technical and operational problems associated with major projects in a climatologically and topographically difficult region with little infrastructure, there are a host of political and financial considerations behind the cautious attitude of the Japanese. The Japanese are well aware that among the Soviet's motives for wanting to get Japan involved is a need to counter or limit Japanese interest in China and to wean Japan away from her preoccupation with regaining her northern territories. Japan does not want to depend on the Soviet for key resources. Moreover, the Japanese are reluctant to do anything in Siberia that would adversely affect Japan's relationship with China or substantially reduce the potential for those relations. In particular, Japan has been wary about development projects that would significantly increase the strategic weight of the Soviet Union in Asia.

In some cases, Japan has made United States participation a condition governing her own. This condition is designed partly to increase the chances of the Soviet living up to her commitments and partly in the hope that such projects will thereby be more palatable to China. Chinese leaders have made it clear that they would be happier if the United States were a partner in such projects. The vast funds required for these projects are generally available only in the American capital market or in capital markets in which the United States is influential; this is another reason for American participation. There have been difficulties in encouraging private American interests to join in the more important projects because of their need of guarantees and Export-Import Bank loans which the U.S. government cannot give so long as its agreement with the Soviet remains moribund.

In the circumstances, perhaps the best that the Soviet can hope is that the Japanese will become sufficiently concerned about the imbalance in their relations with, on the one hand, Peking, and, on the other hand, Moscow, as well as about the fluctuation of relations between Washington and Moscow, to want to make some gestures, albeit without giving anything away on the northern territories. Apart from debate over the northern territories, however, Soviet-Japanese relations are likely to be continually clouded by various incidents whether planned or fortuitous. Difficulties over fishing and other marine resource matters are likely to continue. Indeed, Japan's concern with developing Siberia may well be deflected into projects in Western Asia, following the crescendo of Japanese interest in nurturing good relations with those countries that supply her with life-sustaining oil. If the Soviet Union is snubbed in East Asia, she is going to become more interested in Central and West Asia.

China, for her part, is looking to the export of oil as a means of lifting her economy into the twenty-first century. Until recently, China has been content to export oil from her onshore wells. This onshore oil, although generally low in sulphur content, is high in wax content, necessitating expensive adaptations to refineries in most overseas markets. It has, therefore, been a relatively poor generator of foreign exchange, although oil is already the commodity that China exports to the greatest number of customers and in the greatest quantities. (Even so, she exports only one eighth of her current annual output of oil.)

China's new-found drive to achieve the Four Modernizations demands immense investment and profuse foreign exchange and expertise. Consequently, she is to allow direct government-to-government loans for the first time since the foundation of the People's Republic, along with direct foreign investment on Chinese soil. It should be remembered, however, that China is determined to safeguard her hard-won political and economic sovereignty and, accordingly, is perhaps unlikely to allow foreign investors to have controlling interests in Chinese operations or deeds in perpetuity for assets in China. In addition to overseas loans and investments, China also needs to generate export income to pay for her vast requirements of capital and technology. She is relying upon the export of oil, along with the export of labor-intensive manufactures, such as textiles and clothing, to generate this export income.

It is for these reasons that China's drive for modernization has helped the world to discover China's extensive continental shelf, considered among the most promising areas in the world still unexplored for oil. Viet Nam, too, is hoping to develop offshore oil reserves with the assistance of Canadian, Norwegian, and other foreign companies. Exploration has continued, despite the Kampuchean and Chinese conflicts.

A possibly even greater source of oil than China is on the other side of the Pacific in Mexico. Proven resources of Mexican oil total 40 million barrels, while potential reserves are estimated at 130 million barrels. Like most developing countries, Mexico has a large foreign debt, with one of the highest debt-service ratios in the Third World. Accordingly, she is anxious to use foreign exchange from her oil reserves to service the debt and to pay for imports of capital goods and industrial raw materials. Mexico is, however, a country characterized by gross inequalities and a moderately high rate of inflation. She is not, then, going to allow excessive oil money to accelerate inflation, as has happened to many members of the Organization of the Petroleum Exporting Countries (OPEC), or to generate political and social instability, as in the case of Iran. Mexico thus plans much slower rates of oil production and export than China, although her reserves are probably much more extensive.

These discoveries of oil, or at least this acknowledgment of the existence of oil, in China and Mexico will generate rising living standards in those two countries. Perhaps of more importance, however, they will give the world a little longer to wean itself from its dependence upon oil. The revolution in Iran, it appears, forced a curtailment in the developed world's addictive consumption of oil. It has not, of course, meant a reduction in Iran's underground oil reserves. God is unlikely to produce such an inverse miracle, although we all believe that He was originally an Israeli.

It could be said that it was the Shah's eagerness to satisfy the Western and Japanese thirst for oil that led to his overthrow. At the prevailing rate of exploitation, the Shah had only a few decades of reserves, and during that period he was determined to build a nation that could be ranked among the world's super-powers. Shortages and inflation, the estrangement of the old ruling and merchant classes, the failure to satisfy the new industrial and professional classes, the alienation of traditional skilled farmworkers who found only unskilled employment in the cities, the Shah's associations with Western governments and corporations, and his military megalomania as Britain's successor in the Gulf, spurred by the armament deals with President Nixon and Dr. Kissinger during their visit in 1972—all these contributed to his downfall. But oil is the common factor in all social, political, and strategic questions concerning Iran.

The Chinese and Mexican oil fields on either side of the Pacific will not counteract the effects of the Iranian slowdown. Developments in these three countries will each help, albeit mildly, to extend the days of present Western consumption patterns, which are inevitably numbered. It is important to note that the problem of resource depletion, epitomized by the depletion of oil, is a problem not of the developing nations with their rapid population growth but of the developed nations with their rapid consumption patterns. The annual increase in the population of India, which has three times the population of the United States and eight times the annual population increase of the United States, nonetheless drains only one-third as much of the world's resources as are drained by the annual increase in population of the United States.[1] It is to be hoped that the extension of time that has been granted the West will be used for the development of alternative and safe means of generating energy—reliance upon nuclear energy, when we cannot dispose of its waste or safely control its use, is not a wise course of action—and for the development of energy-efficient means of transporting goods and people. If as much money were spent on research into solar and other energy sources as has been spent on research into oil and nuclear energy, it is unlikely that we would have an energy crisis.

The significant future developments in the area of resources will be as much in the allocation of the resources and in the distribution of the benefits from their exploitation as in their absolute levels. For centuries of colonial and post-colonial patterns of world development, the developed nations of the North Atlantic controlled the extraction, refinement, and distribution of the world's resources. It was the developed nations that made both profits from and use of all that the earth could offer.

In 1973, however, the Third World signaled that this situation could no longer continue unrestrained, when the OPEC nations summarily and substantially increased their prices. It is interesting that the Western media became obsessed with the price rise in oil and ignored the simultaneous quadrupling in the price of wheat, which crippled many developing nations. Perhaps this focusing was justified, for the oil price rise was significant not so much for its effects upon the economies of developed countries—effects that still linger and grow—but for its implications for the struggle between the developed and developing nations that has become the "North-South conflict."

Oil is not the only commodity that has been exploited by the West, giving grossly inadequate recompense to the developing nations and offering opportunities for cartelization by producer nations. Almost every primary product falls into the first category; a number also fall into the second.

Australia, as a major producer of agricultural and then mineral exports, experienced such difficulties, particularly prior to my government's election in December 1972. Australian miners were not getting a fair price for the minerals they exported. There were three reasons for this. First, many of the transnationals could engage in transfer pricing, selling the raw materials at a deflated price to a parent company which would thus reap the excess profits this practice generated. Second, the Australian producers were divided among themselves, each competing for sales, but nearly all facing a cartel of buyers. Third, supplying countries, of which Australia was one, were divided amongst themselves and competing for sales in a manner comparable to supplying companies.

It was discovered that, in the six years from 1967–1968 to 1972–1973, the federal government's total receipts from the principal mining companies in the form of company income tax and mineral royalties were only $268 million. This was less than 14 percent of declared pre-tax profits of those companies, compared with 47 percent of such profits paid in tax by all trading enterprises. Yet, in the same period, the Australian government had paid assistance to these mining companies through income tax concessions to investors, subsidies, bounty payments, and research to the value of $341 million. Instead of contributing to the Consolidated Revenue Fund, as even the highly protected manufacturing sector did, the mining industry had syphoned $55 million—almost $10 million a year—from Australian taxpayers. At the same time, 58 percent of all mining profits after tax were profits payable overseas to direct investors. The combined net revenues to the federal and state governments from the mining industry represented only 20 percent of the value of company profits payable overseas.[2]

My government therefore abolished the taxation concessions that had allowed the mass expatriation of Australian wealth through mining and introduced a system of control of mineral export prices, an act which has been vindicated by the present Minister for Trade and Resources and Deputy Prime Minister in his own attempts to control export prices, despite his party's staunch ideological opposition to such "socialistic practices." He realizes that, if you sell to cartels, you might as well form one. Australia, the world's largest bauxite producer, suggested the International Bauxite Association and, as the second greatest source of iron ore, joined the Association of Iron Ore Exporting Countries (APEF). Inevitably the Philippines will join, as Australia and Papua New Guinea did, the African and South American states in the Intergovernmental Council of Copper Exporting Countries (another French acronym, CIPEC).

Our successors in government, however, have as yet failed to come to grips with the problem of mineral pricing. A contrived boom in aluminium development has been spurred on by the pricing of steaming coal, used for electricity generation and hence aluminium refining, at 60 percent below its export price. It is solely this underpricing—that is, this subsidy by Australian tax-payers to the aluminium industry—that is making many of these new mining projects economic for the multinational miners concerned. Studies carried out for a Federal interdepartmental committee in January 1980 have indicated that, if steaming coal were costed at export parity prices, or electricity tariffs adjusted accordingly, the rate of return on new aluminium smelters would decline to 5 or 6 percent, which would be significantly below their borrowing costs.[3]

The next chapter, on Western Pacific Trade, will deal with the problems developing producers of raw materials in the Western Pacific have had in ensuring an equitable and beneficial pattern of primary product development and trade and of the strategies employed to overcome those difficulties. There is a new bargaining power that developing nations possess that reflects both a new international division of labor and a new consciousness amongst developing nations. It is reflected in the efforts that are being made towards the achievement of a new international economic order. The situation regarding all the resources of the Pacific is extremely complex. Among all the features of the resource picture in the Western Pacific, two seem of paramount importance—the implications of the most complex international negotiations in history, the Third U.N. Conference on the Law of the Sea; and the situation of the Antarctic.

A consideration of these topics might best begin with the recollection that the mariners of Nantucket and New Bedford at the beginning of last century slaughtered the whales and seals of the South and Deep South Pacific. The first whales were caught off the Australian coast in 1791 from a convict transport under Eber Bunker, who had been born in Plymouth, Massachusetts, in 1761 and had gone to London after America's War of National Liberation. He has been called the "father of Australian whaling," Australia's first export industry. (On 6 September 1975, I opened his fully restored home near Sydney.) A Boston ship first visited the new settlement of Sydney in 1793; in the next quarter century as many ships came from Boston as from all other American ports combined. The relations between the Australians and the Americans were not always harmonious, because Eastern Australia fell within the commercial jurisdiction of the British East India Company, which thus could still supervise the commerce of New South Wales although it could no longer supervise the commerce of Massachusetts. The company was as jealous of its rights to the sale of whale oil as it had been of its rights to the sale of tea. In those days the uninational corporations, not the transnationals, were the ogres. There were notable disputes between the settlers in Australia and some of the Americans, such as the two Delano brothers, seal hunters, whose forebears were also forebears of the longest-reigning American president.[4] The Americans used to claim that the conduct of the Australians was what would be expected from convicts, and the Australians rejoined that the conduct of the Americans was no better. The present inhabitants of Cape Barren on Flinders Island in Bass Strait trace their descent equally from the Aboriginal inhabitants of Tasmania and the American sealers and whalers.

American interest in Australian and Antarctic waters continued until the United States liberated California from Mexico and prised the Oregon Territory from Britain and indeed until Americans turned from whale oil to gas for cooking and lighting in the 1850s and discovered petroleum in Pennsylvania 120 years ago. There continued to be closer contacts between this part of the world and Australia until the 1840s than there were again until the 1940s. So much for the background.

In the Law of the Sea, the developing nations have made their most significant breakthrough since OPEC's stance in 1973. In 1953, Peru, with the world's largest fishing industry—for fishmeal production, not human consumption—together with Chile and Ecuador, claimed jurisdiction over the seas for 200 nautical miles from their coastlines. Peru confiscated several Onassis whalers registered in Panama. The claim was repudiated by Britain, the United States, Sweden, Norway, and other maritime powers. In the 1960s, Britain used gunboat diplomacy to resist Iceland's claims to a larger circumference of the sea, with more ignominious results than she had achieved at Suez. Now, a quarter of a century later, the concept of a 200-nautical-mile exclusive economic zone (EEZ) has been accepted by the U.N. Conference attended by 158 nations, great and small, developed and developing.

The Pacific Ocean will most dramatically demonstrate the consequences of the shift in the Law of the Sea from the interests of the naval powers to the interests of coastal and island states. Every nation in the Pacific, except Laos and Bolivia, is such a state. Each of them will have to assert claims to its own EEZ and recognize such claims by others. The Pacific is studded with more archipelagos and atolls than any other ocean. The tropical waters of the South Pacific in particular, as far east as Pitcairn, fall, with very few interstices, within the EEZ of one nation or another. In the eyes of the Law of the Sea the developing countries have achieved parity with the most developed. A minnow-state can have as large a marine zone as a leviathan. Tonga, an extensive archipelago, can approach Japan in importance. Outside its own waters, every nation is likely to be caught in another nation's nets.

The Soviet Union and Japan, with the widest-ranging fleets in the world, will now experience severe limitations on their exploitation of the fishing resources of the Pacific. Already their whaling activities have been doomed by the universal condemnation of mankind. In June 1978, it was interesting to me to find that one of our guides in Leningrad spontaneously mentioned her abhorrence of the whaling in which her nation was still engaged. Since World War I, the Soviet Union has condemned imperialism and, since World War II, Japan has renounced it. For those South Pacific mini-states, however, whose fisheries are their most substantial resource, the great economic imperialists today are the Soviet Union and Japan. Both will now have to demonstrate that they are operating, or will operate, not only in their own interests but also in the interests of all the inhabitants of the Pacific. They may pay license or royalty fees for the privilege of fishing within the EEZs of island states or be persuaded to engage in joint fishing or cannery projects.

It is not at all likely that the super-fleets will be excluded from the waters that fall within the EEZs. The Pacific island nations do not possess the vessels to exploit their waters methodically, although the declaration of the zones will certainly enable them to move a little closer to that situation. Most of the fishing activities within the zones will be carried out by foreign fleets, under license from the coastal states. As a condition for the issuing of licenses, coastal states may require fishing fleets to process a part or the whole of their catch in local plants and to arrange transhipment of catches in local ports. These activities, along with the promotion of local fishing industries and the imposition of license fees, will be significant in generating employment and income in the coastal states.

Already the Japanese have entered into joint cannery projects in Fiji and Solomon Islands and have sent aid missions to Tonga and Western Samoa. Papua New Guinea has banned Japan from her waters unless more acceptable arrangements for access are negotiated. New Zealand briefly did the same after her zone was declared, and the Japanese quickly offered favorable terms. Australia is currently demanding, justifiably, that Japan allow access for Australian fish harvested by Australian companies into Japanese markets equal to the access afforded Australian fish harvested by Japanese companies.

The Soviet Union has offered aid to Tonga and Western Samoa in return for the privilege of building fishing bases but has so far had her approaches rejected, apparently owing to suspicions about her motives. China, though she has no large fishing fleet, is eager to counter Soviet expansionism and accordingly has established embassies in Papua New Guinea, Fiji, and Western Samoa to disseminate agricultural aid and cultural assistance. Australia and New Zealand suddenly increased their aid to the Pacific islands early in 1976 after the Crown Prince of Tonga made a well-publicized visit to the Soviet embassy in Paris. The inhabitants of the Pacific are suddenly finding the warmest of friends among nations they had thought did not even care.

A number of problems, however, arise in the process of finding a new equilibrium in relations amongst maritime and coastal states, particularly in the Pacific. There are grave imbalances in their bargaining powers. This allows a great deal of room for the maritime states to pick off the island states one by one. Differences in license or royalty fees mean that the deep-sea fleets can minimize their expenses by claiming they had caught their load in low-fee or low-royalty zones. Indeed, the lack of surveillance facilities held by the island states presents a severe problem for those states in collecting any royalties from some catches. In such conditions, the arrest and impounding of a few trespassing ships may be insufficient to prevent large-scale poaching of fish within the zones.

I suggest two courses of action. First, licenses to fish inside a zone should be allocated to maritime nation governments, not to individual vessels or companies. The maritime nation governments would then be responsible for regulating their own fleets. This is the emerging pattern. The importance of the fishing industry to the maritime nations' economies would provide a strong incentive for effective regulation. For vessel owners, supervision by their own governments would carry the clout that regulation by foreign governments would not. There is still the problem of Taiwan's large fishing fleet, compounded by the fact that Taipei has successfully lobbied Tonga and Nauru for recognition. (They have not caught up with America. I cannot suggest that the United States acts at all precipitously in these matters. In fact, it took her twice as long to recognize the only government in China after World War II as it took her to recognize the only government in Russia after World War I.) If a Taiwanese ship is apprehended by any of the nations that have recognized Peking as the capital of all China, including the province of Taiwan, the captain may immediately plead that he had made his catch in the zones of Tonga or Nauru.

Second, a common licensing policy is necessary amongst members of the South Pacific Forum. In the discussions to establish a Forum Fisheries Agency, Papua New Guinea vetoed a move for a Forum-wide license to be issued by the Agency, on the argument that it would have created a cumbersome bureaucratic structure. The other nations of the Forum, however, may persuade her that its benefits will outweigh the costs incurred and that a stronger united Forum wields more power than a privileged but isolated Papua New Guinea.

The Forum also contemplated asking the United States and other interested parties to join the Agency, particularly since they could contribute the monitoring capacity of their navies. The United States, however, by refusing to recognize the economic sovereignty of coastal nations over migratory fish, notably tuna, within their EEZs, hardened the attitudes of Forum nations towards her and helped to strengthen their determination to achieve equitable benefits for themselves. The attitude of the United States is a little odd, as presumably she would not allow or encourage unlicensed foreign interests to harvest migratory birds or animals or fish within *her* territorial spaces. If tuna are spawned in an area different from that in which they are harvested, that does not mean there should be laissez-faire exploitation. Rather it means that the coastal state in whose EEZ they spawn should have some predetermined share of the benefits accruing from the harvest. If they spawn in the high seas, then they are part of the "common heritage of mankind," so that part of the royalties from their exploitation should be distributed equitably amongst all mankind. Such migratory habits among fish, however, provide no justification for the unlicensed transgression of national economic sovereignty over living resources in the EEZ. As tuna represent 80 percent of the Pacific fish harvest, the issue is of vital economic consequence for the Pacific island economies.

The large investments required to establish a fleet to harvest migratory fish place such a project beyond the reach of these island nations. Their best, if not only, chance for a fairer slice of the cake lies in the license fees, royalties, and concessions they can wring out of the maritime economies. The opposing stances that have been taken are generating considerable mistrust of developed nation motives amongst the developing nations and are serving to undermine the successful negotiation, adoption, and implementation of a new regime of the sea.

There are also difficulties posed by the demarcation of boundaries. The Conference on the Law of the Sea has been unable to come to any agreement on a uniform basis for determining them. One group of countries favors the general use of a median line between coastlines, taking into account special circumstances, while an opposing group favors the consideration of any and all relevant circumstances, an approach which, it is alleged, will work to the benefit of more powerful nations in negotiations with weaker countries.

There will be special difficulties of demarcation in the Yellow Sea as long as South Korea continues to recognize Taipei as the capital of China. The Taiwan Strait will be claimed by both Peking and Taipei as its exclusive zone. There will be disputes in relation to the Senkaku, Paracel, and Spratly Islands. There has, however, been general agreement that any disputes should be settled by a special council set up for the purpose, or by the International Court of Justice, or by independent arbitration.

The new regime will be important in allowing a greater effort to be made to conserve marine living resources. Stocks of many fish species are rapidly approaching extinction, particularly in the South China Sea. In the short to medium term, then, we may expect a reduction in the extent of fishing in those areas covered by EEZs as coastal nations act to prevent overfishing and depletion of stocks. In the longer term, however, we may expect a greater amount of fishing to occur than would have come about if the previous pattern of unfettered exploitation had persisted; overfishing and near extinction of species would obviously lead to smaller harvests in the long term than would be available under a program for conservations of stocks.

The reverse situation may occur in areas not covered by EEZs. For instance, the Japanese fleet, barred from waters now covered by the U.S.S.R., has increased its activity in the South China Sea and near Japan to the extent that the depletion of stocks there has assumed dangerous proportions. In the Pacific Ocean itself, however, skipjack tuna is not yet being overfished. Except in cases where coastal states ban certain maritime states from their EEZs, either because of unacceptable conditions or resentment of the maritime fleets, there will be no reduction in fishing activity. Indeed, coastal states have an obligation to allow foreign access to their surplus fish, so such bans can only be temporary in nature.

The placing of the responsibility for fisheries in the hands of coastal states and the recognition of the fact that fisheries are not merely the common heritage of trawler operators are vital in leading us towards an effective conservation regime so that future generations will also have access to this important source of food.

There are problems which nonetheless remain with such a regime. For instance, "efficient" management of fisheries in one zone may lead to depletion of stocks in an adjacent zone. There may be problems of coordination, of inexperience, and of inadequate knowledge. For these reasons, the Forum fisheries body is required to oversee the management of South Pacific fisheries. A separate agency may, and should, be established for administration of the waters in and around the South China Sea.

Should these agencies bear ultimate responsibility for fisheries, then they should be funded jointly by maritime and coastal states but consist of representatives of only the coastal states. If the former condition is not fulfilled, the new agency cannot effectively perform functions that are vital for purposes of equity and conservation; if the latter condition is not fulfilled, the coastal states will simply be unwilling to forgo their hard-won sovereignty and see their interests subsumed by developed maritime nations. As a step in the right direction, on 9 and 10 July 1979, the South Pacific Forum drafted a convention establishing a South Pacific Forum Fisheries Agency to be funded one-third by Australia, one-third by New Zealand, and one-thirtieth by each of the 10 other member states of the Forum ranging from Niue (population 4,000) to Papua New Guinea (population 2,800,000). The Agency will collect and disseminate information regarding management, research and marketing and provide "on request . . . assistance in the development of fisheries policies and negotiations and . . . the issue of licenses, the collection of fees or in matters pertaining to surveillance and enforcement."

There is no such competition in fisheries in the South Pacific as there has been for more than three centuries in the North Atlantic. The nations of the Pacific should, therefore, find it easier to achieve the rational and amicable conservation and development of resources of the Pacific by concluding fisheries conventions.

Extensive multilateral conventions have been used in the past to govern the exploitation of fisheries, with varying degrees of success. The International Convention for the Northwest Atlantic Fisheries of 1949 involved 15 nations including the United States, Britain, Japan, and the Soviet Union. It established the International Commission for the Northwest Atlantic Fisheries, empowered to research and regulate fisheries in the Northwest Atlantic. The form of regulation for many years primarily involved minimum mesh-size regulations but, as a conservation weapon, it was ineffective because of the extensive scale of the distant water fleets of the Soviet Union and other nations. Consequently, overall quotas were finally agreed to for haddock, flounder, and salmon.

The North-East Atlantic Fisheries Convention of 1959 was negotiated by 14 nations, including Britain and the Soviet Union. It established the North-East Atlantic Fisheries Commission, which makes recommendations to member states, mainly regarding minimum mesh sizes and minimum fish sizes. Because it has been unable to exact recommendations regarding national quotas, it has been unsuccessful in keeping exploitation of many stocks to the level of maximum sustainable yield; depletion has resulted.

A number of treaties and commissions covered the fisheries of the Pacific before the re-specification of the Law of the Sea. These included the Indo-Pacific Fisheries Commission, the International North Pacific Fisheries Commission, multilateral treaties such as those between the United States, Korea, and Japan, between

Canada, Korea, and Japan, and between Mexico and the United States, as well as bodies such as the International Whaling Commission and the Inter-American Tropical Tuna Commission. In time, as whaling is brought to a halt, the International Whaling Commission will cease to exist. Most of these other conventions and commissions are becoming dead letters as the new Law of the Sea regime comes into effect. Their only utility is in the dissemination of information.

The sensible objective for the nations of the Pacific should be a Pacific Fisheries Convention. All the insular and littoral states of the Pacific should be parties to it. It should recognize the redistribution of income and resources represented by the new Law of the Sea regime. The convention would serve to stabilize and consolidate the new structure of allocation and management the regime implies. Without a convention, there may be a rapid deterioration in stocks of fish that are not located within the EEZ of any nation, comparable to what has already occurred in some areas near Japan's coast and in the South China Sea. The conservation of food resources for our descendants must be a fundamental objective in formulating policy regarding international fisheries. Such a new convention governing the harvesting of Pacific fish, involving both coastal and distant water states, is proposed in Article 64 of the Revised Informal Composite Negotiating Text, the draft convention for the new Law of the Sea.

It is important to realize that the new Law of the Sea is a vital link in the resolution of the current North-South conflict and is perhaps the single most important step that has had any degree of success in achieving a New International Economic Order. Like the three Latin American countries that originally declared a 200-mile territorial waters claim in 1953, the majority of countries that stand to benefit from the new Law of the Sea are developing countries. This is particularly the situation in the Pacific where all the countries are developing countries except Japan, the Soviet Union, the United States, Canada, Australia, and New Zealand. There will be not only a redistribution of wealth in the Pacific but also a redistribution of power, as the developing coastal nations will be able to use their power to regulate fishing activities as a means of prising concessions from developed countries on other economic issues.

The Third U.N. Conference on the Law of the Sea (UNCLOS III) is concerned with the sea bed as well as the sea, with vertical as well as horizontal jurisdiction. The Conference still has to agree on the details of such issues as the exploitation of the unquantified amounts of potato-size nodules of cobalt, nickel, manganese, and copper lying on the floor of the oceans and, it seems, particularly of the Pacific Ocean. This issue raises in an acute form the conflict between the wealth and skills of the 6 to 10 most industrialized nations and the aspirations of the rest of the world. It is the crux of the North-South conflict.

The Third U.N. Conference on the Law of the Sea has agreed to set up an Authority which will be involved in the extraction of minerals from the deep sea bed, through the operations of an Enterprise established under the Authority's jurisdiction. Conflict has centered around the role of the Authority in deep sea bed exploitation. Many developing countries want the Enterprise to be the only body allowed to mine the sea bed, in order that the benefits may be equitably distributed between developing and developed nations. They perceive the riches of the ocean's depths as being part of the "common heritage of mankind." On the other hand, developed nations want private companies to be able to mine the sea bed independent of the Enterprise. It appears that the "parallel" system of exploitation, as agreed upon in the Eighth Session of UNCLOS III, is the most desirable compromise. Under this system, private companies or national operators will, if they satisfy financial and technical requirements set by the Authority, be able to delimit a particular area of sea bed for exploitation. The operator will mine one-half of this area and the Authority will mine the other half, while being supplied with sufficient technology and finance to make its operations viable. This last point is vital, for, if the Authority does not have expertise and resources comparable to the private and national operators, it will be unable to compete with them, and the developing nations will consequently receive minimal benefits.

It is also necessary that there be control over the exploitation of sea-bed minerals so that land-based producers of these minerals will not find the markets for these exports depressed because of oversupply. Thus, the rate of mining of manganese nodules is likely to be tied to the worldwide demand for nickel. Without these controls, the developing nations' aspirations for international commodity agreements could be undermined.

At the same time, as attempts are being made to define an international convention for a sea-bed regime that is acceptable to all states—143 nations are involved in the Conference on the Law of the Sea—other attempts are being made to pre-empt the outcome of the Conference, which will undermine its universal acceptability. The U.S. House of Representatives has passed legislation that would allow American companies to mine the deep sea bed. Japan and the European Community member states are apparently planning similar unilateral action. Not only does such action jeopardize the chances for a successful negotiation and acceptance of a sea-bed regime, but it also serves to redistribute wealth and foreign exchange away from the developing countries which are badly in need of means of overcoming their overseas debt. During the Resumed Eighth Session of UNCLOS III (August 1979), further progress was made particularly regarding the financial terms of mining contracts with private or national operators and the financing of the Enterprise. There was still, however, no agreement upon whether and how a transfer of technology to the Enterprise was to be guaranteed, on whether there would be production controls and/or assured market access for the deep-sea miners, and on what would be the decision-making procedure in the executive (the Council) of the Assembly.

Although the emerging Law of the Sea regime has not evolved as the developing countries would have wished, they are having more success in this area than in negotiations affecting the established trading regime of the world. The question as to whether the new regime can come into force prior to any unilateral legislation depends upon whether the rate of progress in moving towards a deep-sea-bed regime can exceed the rate of disaffection of Western corporations and hence of Western legislators.

The new Law of the Sea also has implications for the protection of the marine environment. For the first time since the takeoff in the transport of petroleum and crude oil by seagoing vessels, the right of a port state to institute proceedings against a foreign vessel for discharge offenses on the high seas has been recognized. While, however, port and coastal states may exercise authority when pollution has already occurred, they have little power to exercise authority before the event. Thus, the right to regulate design and construction remains the prerogative of the flag states. Yet many Western ships, mainly owned in the United States and Japan, have flown under flags of convenience precisely to avoid safety or labor regulations or taxation of various forms. Most recently, a large number of South Korean shipowners changed their registration to Liberia to avoid minimum-wage legislation that had been passed in Korea.

Not surprisingly, the new Law of the Sea regime will require that some "genuine link," usually involving ownership, should exist betweeen the ship and the state whose flag she carries. There are, however, no specific provisions in the new regime for safety and pollution standards but only exhortations that states should cooperate in these mattters. The explosion of the *Betelgeuse* in Bantry Bay was caused by the inflammable imbroglio of oil vapor and air. Such explosions can be prevented only by the use of inert blanketing, whereby inert nitrogen is pumped into the ship's tanks to replace the oil that is being pumped out; yet only 20 percent of the world's oil tankers are equipped with inert blanketing. National and international action is necessary to prevent such an incident recurring in a more populous urban port. The common standards that are set by the Intergovernmental Maritime Consultative Organization (IMCO) are adhered to by only a limited number of states. The 1973 International Convention on Prevention of Pollution from Ships, which provides for more extensive protective measures and regulations than currently exist, has been ratified by only two nations and has not yet entered into force. The current provisions for safety and pollution control are generally inadequate, since IMCO is dominated by the maritime states with an interest in keeping costs as low as possible.

The Law of the Sea also has implications for Antarctica. There is no such strategic conflict between nations in the Antarctic as there has been for more than three decades between NATO and the Soviet Union in the Arctic. In 1909, British explorers claimed possession of tracts of Antarctica and, between 1911 and 1914, an Australian expedition laid claim to further discoveries. The Australian Antarctic Territory, comprising former British and Australian claims, was proclaimed in 1936. It covers an area of 2.5 million square miles, almost half the land surface of Antarctica, and is five-sixths the size of the Australian continent. Other claimants to Antarctic territory include New Zealand, as an heir of Britain, Chile and Argentina, as heirs of Spain—John Paul II is now called on to interpret the arbitration of Alexander VI—and Norway and France, as discoverers in their own right. The United States and the Soviet Union have refused to recognize any declarations of sovereignty, claiming that there can be no sovereignty where there has been no occupation and settlement. In 1958, the International Geophysical Year, the Soviet Union permanently established a number of scientific bases in territory claimed by Australia. Realizing she could not make them go away, Australia announced she would let them stay, since she believed in free scientific development in Antarctica and the banning of all military activity in the region. The British and New Zealand governments, in similar situations, generously and simultaneously concurred.

In 1959, 12 nations signed the Antarctic Treaty. It guaranteed the use of Antarctica for peaceful purposes only, the facilitation of scientific research and international scientific cooperation there, and the preservation and conservation of its living resources. The original signatories were the 7 claimants to territory plus the United States, the Soviet Union, Belgium, Japan and South Africa,

and these 12 together with Poland, which signed in 1961, attend
the biennial Antarctic Treaty Consultative Meetings. The tenth
meeting was held in Washington D.C. in September and October
1979. Seven other nations have signed the treaty but are not yet
consultative parties: Czechoslovakia (1962), Denmark (1965), the
Netherlands (1967), Romania (1971), East Germany (1974),
Brazil (1975), and West Germany (1978). The Treaty does not
deal with the exploitation of Antarctica's resources. After the
lapse of twenty years, it is no longer possible to leave that question to 20 nations and mostly developed nations at that.

The worldwide assumption of 200-mile EEZs highlights the
problem of sovereignty when there is no permanent settlement.
Any Australian assertion of jurisdiction over the seas within 200
nautical miles of the Antarctic coast would not be recognized by
any nation in the Pacific region except, possibly, New Zealand.
The Australian government has presently stepped up activity in
Antarctica, commencing an air service to the continent that had
previously been reached only by chartered ships, in an effort to
demonstrate its latent and increasing interest in Antarctica.

The new Law of the Sea would have little effect upon the
Antarctic status quo, if the only motivation for involvement were
scientific research. Now, however, the whole world is turning its
gaze to the Antarctic, looking towards the resources to be found
in its cold, harsh terrain. Underneath the sheets of ice are unquantified mineral reserves and oil for which the West lusts;
beneath the waves of the southern ocean swim salty krill.

The potential yield of krill is probably equivalent to the present
worldwide yield of fish. The Soviet Union, Japan, Taiwan, and
Poland have been investigating the exploitation of this protein-
rich crustacean for a decade, although the annual harvest has
never exceeded 0.5 percent of the estimated potential catch.
Cod, whiting, and squid are also potential food sources in great
quantities.

There are problems with krill. It deteriorates rapidly unless
processed, requiring "factory ships" large enough to incorporate
processing machinery. Its saltiness is also an obstacle to marketing.

More important, however, is the delicate ecology of the ocean from which it comes. Krill is a crucial part of a food chain, feeding on plankton and being in turn the main diet of whales, squid, and fish, while fish in turn are the main source of food for seals and penguins. An over-harvesting of krill could lead to a rapid decline in numbers amongst animals further along the food chain, although mankind has apparently tried to pre-empt this by hunting the blue, white, and humpback whales to near extinction. If the imminent cessation of whaling causes an increase in the whale population, more krill will be consumed and the total supply reduced.

There is some anticipation that mining ventures in the Antarctic will become technically and economically feasible around the turn of the century. Recoverable oil reserves have been thought to total anything between 10 and 45 billion barrels, although detailed exploration has yet to take place. Most of this is believed to be under the seas surrounding the continent. Iron ore and low-quality coal have been identified in apparent abundance. In the next twenty years, we can expect commercial prospecting to determine what mineral resources lie under the Antarctic ice. It would be extremely surprising if a continent of this size is not found to contain vast quantities of certain minerals.

There are, of course, problems with mining. It goes almost without saying that the gusty, frigid conditions and the thick ice will make exploitation a far more difficult task than on any other continent, and it is unlikely that this will take place until diminishing world supplies of minerals force prices upwards. Mining could be very hazardous; a collision with an iceberg, with an average displacement of 100,000 metric tons, would obliterate any oil-drilling installation. A major danger is that significant oil spillages could result in changing ground temperatures and ice levels and consequently might affect worldwide sea levels, to say nothing of effects upon the Antarctic ecosystem. Substantial human settlement or tourism would generate considerable human and non-human wastes which, because of the cold, would degrade only very slowly and hence have indeterminate impacts on the Antarctic environment.

A final resource, one that is not as unimportant as it first sounds, is ice. Some Australian businessmen and academic scientists have been seriously investigating the prospects of towing icebergs to arid areas as a source of fresh water.

There are further problems that pervade the exploitation of both living and non-living resources in the Antarctic, and these target on the question of who is to benefit from these vast resources. The parties to the Antarctic Treaty, realizing the great potential of Antarctic resources, have attempted to begin the drafting of a regime for their exploitation. They claim that they have successfully managed Antarctica amongst themselves until now, and therefore they expect they will continue to do so in the future ad infinitum. Such assertions and expectations ignore the fact that the Treaty was designed to promote scientific research in the Antarctic with the express purpose of maintaining the status quo in all other areas (territorial claims, nuclear testing, military usage, and so on). The exploitation of the Antarctic resources will represent an immense *change* in the Antarctic status quo and will be something in which the Treaty parties have had no experience whatsoever. Granting the parties to a scientific treaty the right to determine a resources regime has all the virtue of leaving to the U.S. Army Corps of Engineers all responsibility for health, social welfare, and town planning in the Mississippi catchment.

A convention signed by the treaty parties cannot be expected to gain compliance from non-treaty parties interested in Antarctic marine resources. The absurdity of any claim by the treaty parties that they can efficiently manage the Antarctic for the benefit of mankind is demonstrated by the fact that any non-parties wishing to involve themselves in the negotiations of this marine resources conservation regime must first be invited to do so. As almost all the treaty parties are developed countries, this is a less-than-subtle means of excluding developing countries—three quarters of mankind—from the development of an Antarctic resource regime.

Over the past few years, the consultative parties have discussed a regime for the exploitation of living and non-living Antarctic resources. Their hesitancy to proceed, due to the difficulties encountered from the inappropriateness of the Antarctic Treaty as a means for developing such a regime, is tempered by a haste to present the world with a *fait accompli* before the nations of the Third World can demand an equitable regime. The developing countries are currently preoccupied with other issues, but Antarctica has been an issue since India attempted to raise it in the United Nations in 1956 and 1958, prior to the conclusion of the Antarctic Treaty. More recently, Papua New Guinea and Sri Lanka have supported the idea of an international, rather than a multilateral, regime for Antarctica.

There is much doubt as to whether a regime could be negotiated by the consultative parties. There are problems of overlapping claims to territory. Who appropriates the royalties in areas that are unclaimed? If the royalties are to be divided evenly, is it amongst only those parties with territorial claims? If so, is it in proportion to their claims? If not, what proportion do the non-territorial parties get? What would be the level of royalties? How is technology to be shared amongst countries ranging in population size from the U.S.A. and the U.S.S.R. to Norway and Argentina? How is the convention to be enforced? How is an oil installation to be guarded without militarizing the Antarctic? Even if a regime could develop out of this set of contradictions it would be challenged by the rest of the world. Its basis in international law would be extremely shaky.

The appropriate regime from which an Antarctic resources regime will be developed cannot be an old scientific cooperation treaty between a dozen nations or a score. It will be the Law of the Sea regime which will regulate and allocate the benefits flowing from the "common heritage of mankind" in this area. The consultative parties cannot even agree amongst themselves who owns what, and if they ever do agree it will be a spurious agreement indeed.

A global regime for the exploitation of Antarctic resources is inevitable because it is the only possibility that is internationally acceptable and equitable. An international conference on Antarctica must follow the U.N. Conference on the Law of the Sea, so that sufficient time is allowed to develop a regime before exploitation becomes a reality. The United States might feel inhibited because of her own economic involvement and domestic pressures in taking an initiative for a Pacific Fisheries Convention. On the other hand, because of her refusal to make or recognize territorial claims, she is admirably placed to take an initiative for the internationalization of Antarctica.

The opportunity before us is one that has rarely been afforded to humanity: the opportunity to examine carefully and thoroughly the ecological and economical impact of harnessing the living and non-living resources of an area before we actually set out to harness them. By investigating the structure of life in the Antarctic ecosystem we can and must prevent a repetition of the haphazard exploitation of the seas that has been the pattern of history. By negotiating the structure of a regime for the exploitation of the resources of the Antarctic we can and must attempt to make the grotesque inequalities and conflicts between the North and the South a feature of history past.

With the world approaching a dual crisis involving resource depletion and deepening conflicts between the developed and Third World, it is vital that international agreements be made for ensuring effective conservation and equitable distribution of the resources of the Pacific region from the Antarctic to the Arctic. In the Pacific, with its multitude of nation states, large and small, rich and poor, ancient and modern, we have a crucible in which mankind can draw up a significant and rational program to conserve and exploit its common heritage of resources.

TWO

Western Pacific Trade

A century ago, all the nations in the Western Pacific except China, Japan, Korea, and Siam had come to be governed from imperial capitals in Lisbon, the Hague, Madrid, London, Paris, and Berlin; and China's ports were controlled by foreigners. In the first half of this century, Korea and Taiwan came to be ruled by Japan, the Philippines by the United States, and Papua New Guinea by Australia. These empires had divided up the peoples of Polynesia, Micronesia, and Melanesia, and the numerous peoples of East and South Asia amongst themselves and had oriented the Western Pacific economies towards production of goods such as rubber, cotton, tea, sugar, jute, and palm oil—on land formerly available for domestic food production—for the patron-nation economies. Even Australia's export economy was geared towards the North Atlantic. She used to produce agricultural and, to a certain extent, those mineral products required in North America and Europe and particularly in the mother country, Great Britain.

Since 1945, however, the Japanese, American, British, Dutch, Australian, and Portuguese empires have successively dissolved, and China has become mistress in her own household. All the peoples of Asia, of North and South America, of Australia and New Zealand, and 4.1 million of the 4.6 million inhabitants of the islands of the South Pacific have their own governments which may, to varying degrees, be more likely to serve the interests of their people than were the colonial governments. With the shackles of the imperial economies removed, the economic and political interdependence of the Pacific region's nations has grown symbiotically.

Decolonization is the single most obvious factor responsible for the growing interdependence of the Pacific region economies, but several developments since decolonization have been important in hastening or hampering mutuality. One of the trends that has made for a greater intraregional interdependence has been developments in technology. Rapid progress in marine transportation means that it is now significantly cheaper than land transportation. Thus, it is less expensive to ship goods from Yokohama to California than it is to transport them by land from Illinois to California, just as it is less expensive to ship goods to Eastern Siberia from Australia than it is to railroad them to Eastern Siberia from Moscow. The present Chinese government is the first in history to have avoided famines; it finds it easier to provide grains for much of the coastal population by sea than by land transport. Innovations in the fields of containerization and bulk freight are important in developing trade in the Western Pacific, since the larger proportion of its commerce must cross the vast seas. Progress in satellites and submarine coaxial cables has greatly assisted communications in the Pacific region. Submarine cables have recently been opened between Japan and the United States, between Japan and China, between Japan, the Philippines, and Hong Kong, and between the Philippines and Singapore. A Singapore-Indonesia cable is about to be laid. The MARISAT, INTERSAT, and VENUS satellite systems are helping increase the volume and reduce the cost of communications. Furthermore, the relaxation of the international airline cartel and the introduction of cheaper air fares will stimulate the Pacific economy in the fashion though not to the degree that the completion of the transcontinental railroads stimulated the U.S. economy.

The second development that has increased interdependence has been the resurrection of Japan from the ashes of her wartime devastation to become the second largest market economy in the world. Japan's industrial growth generated a tremendous demand for raw materials, which thereby laid the conditions for large-scale, profitable investment within the region in the extractive industries, particularly in Australia. This led to important changes in the structure of the Australian economy, although for many years Australia's taxation system minimized the gain to Australian welfare by allowing mining companies to ship both the minerals and the profits overseas while paying no more than token taxes. This was remedied in 1973 by my government, but our successors have sought to reintroduce the concessions which they think lured the mineral speculators of the 1960s. Thailand, Malaysia, the Philippines, and Indonesia are all relatively well-endowed with natural resources, and close to Japan. Japan's demand for foodstuffs and raw materials, principally satisfied by the nations to her south and southwest, has thus been a major source of stimulus to regional trade and to the export economies of these nations.

More recently, structural change in the Japanese economy following the liberalization of trade and payments and the appreciation of the yen in 1971 created a strong demand for labor-intensive manufactures produced in the region, as the Japanese economy shifted towards more technologically advanced, capital-intensive production. Between 1971 and 1974, Japan had increased her share in worldwide labor-intensive manufactured imports two and a half times.[1] This process of restructuring was interrupted by the oil crisis of 1974, following which import restrictions and deflationary monetary policies were implemented in an attempt to curtail the sudden balance-of-payments deficit.

By 1976, Japan's famous balance-of-payments surplus had developed in response to the over-reaction of economic policy to the oil crisis measures. In the meantime, she had learnt some important lessons. She had learnt to concentrate industrial expansion upon undertakings that would make light demands upon natural resources, in particular oil. She had also learnt to avoid expansion of industries that had detrimental effects upon the physical environment. She was thus going to concentrate upon the expansion of industries that made efficient use of her highly skilled work force; she was to develop more "knowledge-intensive" or "skill-intensive" industries. Thus, when trade was again liberalized, the yen was again appreciated, and structural change revived, there developed a renewed strong demand for labor-intensive manufactures which greatly stimulated the nearby economies of developing East Asia. The demand for minerals, however, has not increased proportionately, and so the stimulus to Australia's mineral trade with Japan has not been so powerful. Australia's mineral exports will increasingly be destined for other countries in the East Asia region.

The growth of Japan has also led to her emergence as a major source of investment in the region. By the end of 1976, Japan was responsible for roughly 34 percent of all outstanding foreign investment in developing East Asia, excluding investment in Indonesian oil, compared with a figure of 25 percent for American investment. Seven years earlier, Japan's figure was only a third that of the United States.[2]

The ascendancy of Japan has coincided with the stagnation and introversion of Europe. In the three years from 1974 to 1977, Europe's real total gross domestic product (GDP) increased at an average rate of only 0.5 percent per annum, compared with annual rates of 1.6 percent in North America and 7.6 percent in East Asia and the Pacific.[3] Europe has thus provided a dwindling market for goods produced in the Pacific region, while the European Community's protectionist trade policies have actively discouraged the sale of Pacific goods in the Community. The decline and fall of the great empires formerly dutifully serving the capital cities of Europe caused the European powers to conclude that their economic future lay within their own region. This realization has engendered and enhanced the European Community and, by default, facilitated interdependence in the Western Pacific.

A perhaps more important force intensifying regional interdependence in the Western Pacific has been the direction of economic policies in the nations of East Asia. These policies have involved the deliberate adoption of industrialization strategies and the reorientation of the economies to the export of manufactured goods. In the immediate post-war period, developing Asian countries desired above all to be able to renounce their dependency upon the imperial capitals and become self-sufficient. Thus, throughout the 1950s, industrialization through import substitution was encouraged, and substantial protective barriers were erected. The reliance on domestic markets meant that, after the initial phase of expansion of import-replacing industries, industrial growth began to be constrained by the relative smallness of the home economies.

Meanwhile, Australia was embarking on a massive immigration program to provide labor for broad-based manufacturing industries that were being developed behind protective barriers, usually by overseas-owned corporations. In this way, Australian consumers came to succor large textile and automobile manufacturing industries, the latter comprising no fewer than 5 manufacturers—General Motors, Ford, Chrysler, Nissan, and Toyota—for a population of only 14 million; only the United States produced a greater range of models.

From the late 1950s, there was growing disillusionment amongst developing East Asian nations with the consequences of policies based on import substitution: employment benefits were not up to expectations, growth prospects were poor (because of the inability to export), dependence on imported capital equipment and raw materials adversely affected the balance of payments, and the agricultural sector was disadvantaged by the high costs in the manufacturing sector. More important, the import-substitution policies encouraged industries that were not based on the comparative advantage of Asian countries at that time. Many of the countries were confronted with high rates of growth in their labor force.

These countries retained the legacy of their colonial days in the form of land devoted to crops that were designed for consumption abroad rather than at home. As a long-term trend, the prices of the exports of these countries deteriorated vis-à-vis the price of their imports. Between 1954 and 1962, the buying power of primary goods declined 18 percent, so that the terms of trade of the developing countries vis-à-vis the developed countries fell 19 percent in this period.[4] As the declining terms of trade generated balance-of-payments difficulties, countries often initiated deflationary economic policies which would encourage the diversion of resources, particularly land, towards export-oriented primary industries and increase the dependency upon imported food. This pressure, along with that from increasing population in developing Asian countries and that from the collusion of grain traders and the U.S. Department of Agriculture under Public Law 480,[5] led to Asia changing from being a net exporter of grain to the order of 2 million metric tons in the mid-1930s to a net importer to the order of 17 million metric tons by 1960.[6] More important, the prices of primary exports fluctuated rapidly, making planning and orderly development virtually impossible in countries that were dependent upon the fortunes of a few commodities, fortunes over which they had little or no control.

Today, as then, the developing countries are in an unenviable position when they rely upon the export of primary goods. We now find, for instance, that, while consumers in the developed world pay $200 billion a year for the major primary commodities exported by developing nations, only $30 billion of this accrues to the producers in the developing nations.[7] The rest accrues to the packers, shippers, insurers, ripeners, wholesalers, and retailers of the industrial nations. It is no wonder, then, that the developing nations are attempting to institute their own national shipping lines so that they may have greater control over the distribution and economic return of their exports.

This twin problem I have described—the inherent inefficiencies of industrialization oriented towards import substitution and the often counterproductive effects of agriculture oriented towards exports—resulted in a general shift in policy emphasis to export-oriented industrialization. In 1958, Taiwan implemented a policy package aimed at encouraging the expansion of labor-intensive exports. South Korea followed suit during the 1960s. The small island economies of Hong Kong and Singapore had little choice in their approach to industrialization, and the growth of manufacturing production in these economies was, from the beginning, oriented towards overseas markets.

At the same time, East Asian nations began to change their attitudes towards foreign investment. In the early 1950s, nationalistic sentiment prevented large-scale foreign investment in all countries except Taiwan. Between 1958 and 1960, however, three members of the Association of South-East Asian Nations (ASEAN)—Thailand, Malaysia and Singapore—enacted legislation encouraging the inflow of foreign capital. South Korea and the other two members of ASEAN—the Philippines and Indonesia—proceeded similarly in 1966 and 1967. In the ASEAN countries, apart from Singapore, investment was concentrated in the expansion of domestic-oriented manufacturing industries, a process that led to a wasteful and eventually quite visible misallocation of resources. Malaysia took steps to increase the export orientation of the industrial sector, while the Philippines and Thailand made tentative but similar moves. In the early 1970s, restrictions were made to shift investment to selected export-oriented industries. South Korea in particular has concentrated on the import of foreign technology rather than of foreign capital. Among the ASEAN countries, the proportion of exports that were manufactured rose by four percentage points, or 24 percent, between 1971 and 1974.[8] Indonesia alone among the East Asian market economies has maintained protective import-substitution policies. Her emphasis on the production of capital-intensive goods, together with her dependence on oil as her principal export, has had little beneficial effect upon employment. For Indonesia, foreign investment has been far from a success. Despite having the second highest level of foreign investment per capita amongst the ASEAN nations (behind Singapore) and the second highest proportion of foreign investment to GDP amongst all developing East Asian nations (behind Singapore) her economy is the slowest to perform. The reluctance of her government to direct foreign investment to trade-oriented activities and its inability to restructure the economy have meant that a substantial level of overseas ownership of Indonesian industry and resources has come about without a commensurate increase in the welfare of the Indonesian people.

What we have seen, then, are changes in the attitudes to foreign investment and in the patterns of foreign investment in the Western Pacific. The same pressure has been evident in Australia. Foreign investment in the 1950s and 1960s, largely the responsibility of American firms, took place in industries that were aimed at consumption in the domestic market. This investment was carried out behind the protection of high tariff and non-tariff barriers against import competition. During the late 1960s and early 1970s, foreign investment in Australia assumed a second character. This was evident in the lavish investment in minerals to be shipped overseas for processing, often in Japan. This form of investment was trade-oriented as opposed to the anti-trade-oriented investment that had characterized much of manufacturing. Nevertheless, it created significant problems. It diverted capital away from manufacturing, thus retarding the rate of investment in productive plant and machinery. It raised the exchange rate, thus making export-oriented manufactures less competitive overseas and imported components more expensive. Profits were being repatriated on an immense scale, while minimal direct or indirect employment benefits were generated. Until my government persuaded Japanese buyers to adopt a more generous and responsible attitude, Australia faced the same problems in the export of its minerals as developing nations did.

Australia has still to come to terms with her high levels of unemployment and high rates of protection. A body of thought is growing, however, that Australia, too, must restructure her economy. The eventual pattern will be one in which manufacturing industry becomes more specialized, skill-intensive, and export-oriented. In addition, we may expect to see more resource-based manufacturing in Australia, particularly as the comparative advantage drifts further away from Japan. In line with these developments, of course, will be advocacy for lowering of barriers to Asian imports.

A recent and perhaps pioneering instance of trade-oriented foreign investment in manufacturing has been the approval of General Motors' plans to build a four-cylinder engine plant as part of the "world car" concept. The world car is a possible symbol of a predicted transformation of the pattern of overseas investment towards trade-oriented activity. This pattern has been particularly characteristic of Japanese firms, which have used overseas investment as a means of accommodating the rapid changes in Japan's own comparative advantage.

What is best for General Motors may not be best for the nations of the world, however. As U.S. and Japanese automobile manufacturers set up operations in more and more countries of the Western Pacific, the United States, Japan, and the nations concerned may well want to regulate the operations of the companies in each country. The extent and place of manufacture and the frequency and price of models cannot be left to unilateral decisions in Detroit. The companies may dangle the prospect of automotive industries before the Pacific countries one by one and set them against each other, as so many companies do to the states or provinces in a federation. A step to prevent this situation has been taken by the United States and her first and largest economic colony, Canada. On 16 January 1965, the President and Prime Minister made an Agreement Concerning Automotive Products; a few days earlier, each manufacturer sent a letter of undertaking to the Canadian government. Pacific nations with U.S. automobile plants should now act likewise. Canada was afraid she would become the Moon to America's Earth; the developing countries of the Pacific do not want to become the satellites to her Jupiter. There should be more such agreements, and they should be multilateral. The Canadian agreement needs review; all such agreements should provide for periodic reviews.

This pattern of world investment will give developing countries—and countries like Australia—a far greater say in determining the incidence of the benefits of international investment. Whereas, previously, a transnational corporation would threaten a government that it would close down a subsidiary operation if it did not stay profitable, such a corporation will find this threat very hard to carry out when the subsidiary is not an autonomous unit but a vital link in the vertical structure of the company, without which the other operations may falter or even collapse. In addition, developing nations are acting more and more cooperatively and cohesively, and it is becoming less and less possible for transnational corporations to play off one country against another. Countries that make substitutable components should, and will, be able to make agreements preventing such playing off of one country against another.

Whereas once the transnationals formed the cartels that held sway over the world, the developing countries are beginning to form producer cartels that will themselves hold sway over the world. The earliest, most effective, and best known of these cartels is the Organization of the Petroleum Exporting Countries (OPEC). It will not, however, be the last.

For economic growth in developing East Asia to be sustainable and equitable, the decision-making power regarding investment must rest with the developing countries themselves, rather than with the foreign corporations or governments. The countries of the region must cooperate to escape being picked off one by one by the transnational corporations. Ultimately, there may be a conference and convention involving those developing countries and developed countries on the periphery of the international economy—including Australia, New Zealand, and the countries of developing East Asia—that would reach agreement on the conditions under which foreign investment is to be accepted. Countries will, as indeed they must, enact legislation requiring greater disclosure of information by transnationals, democratization of management, and direct involvement of the national government in the planning of investment, capital raising, and currency flows as a condition for renewing those companies' charters to operate within the countries concerned.

Trade, not just aid, is the means by which the developing East Asian countries will achieve economic growth. Only Sweden, the Netherlands, Norway, and Denmark among the nations in the Development Assistance Committee (DAC) of the Organization for Economic Cooperation and Development (OECD) have fulfilled their 1974 promise to raise official development assistance to 0.7 percent of the donor nations' gross domestic product. Sweden expends 1.0 percent of her GDP on official development assistance. Australia's contribution has fallen to 0.45 percent under the present administration.[10] It is sadly noteworthy that, while the United States donated 2.5 percent of her GDP for the reconstruction of Europe under the Marshall Plan, she has seen fit to earmark only a tenth of this amount for the reconstruction of developing countries. Some commentators even assert that the only way countries can get massive economic aid from the United States these days is to threaten action that would endanger American oil supplies.

Indeed, the oil-producing developing countries of OPEC are rapidly becoming more helpful to the developing nations of East and South Asia than are the industrialized Development Assistance Committee nations. In Asia between 1974 and 1976, the ratio of official aid from the OPEC countries to official aid from DAC countries rose from 17 percent to 48 percent.[11] In 1977, OPEC aid to all developing countries represented 2.0 percent of the OPEC nations' GDP, compared with 0.3 percent of the GDP of the DAC nations.[12] For some OPEC nations, the figure was particularly high; 10.1 percent of the United Arab Emirates' GDP was devoted to aid, as was 7.4 percent of Qatar's GDP and 5.7 percent of Saudi Arabia's GDP.[13] Although OPEC aid to Asian countries is significantly less than their increased oil bills, the establishment of the OPEC Special Fund in August 1976 and its likely expansion may foreshadow the reversal of this situation. In Vienna in January 1980, the OPEC finance ministers agreed in principle to convert the Special Fund into an OPEC Bank, a permanent, legally constituted institution with a pool of capital similar to the World Bank.

Official aid payments from DAC countries have not even been sufficient to cover the debt-service payments of developing countries. In 1976, the debt-service payments of the five member nations of ASEAN were $1.4 billion, over 70 percent higher than the official development assistance those countries received from DAC nations that year.[14] This pattern of debts exceeding aid characterizes the developing nations of East and South Asia as much as it characterizes the developing nations of the world.

Trade provides the ASEAN countries with thirty times the foreign currency that official development aid provides. Furthermore, a great deal of foreign "aid"—the term is generally bastardized to denote any flow, governmental or commercial, from developed to developing countries—is often tied to the purchase of particular goods from the donor country, which is not always in the long-term interests of efficiency in the recipient country. Trade—in manufactured goods—is providing by default the only avenue by which developing Asian countries can ameliorate their problems. This does not preclude my saying that the industrialized nations must review and upgrade their embarrassingly small aid programs.

What is happening, in fact, is that the East Asia region is promising to become the most rapid growth region in the world throughout the rest of this century. According to the preliminary figures issued in the World Bank Report of 1979, the real rate of growth in GDP in 1978 was higher in the East Asia and Pacific region (at 8.9 percent) than in the industrialized countries (3.6 percent) or any other regions of developing countries, among which the average was 5.2 percent growth. The same pattern was true of per capita GDP and manufacturing production.[15] At the same time, the East Asia and Pacific region had been the most successful in containing the growth rates of their populations. This comes as no great surprise: the fertilities of the populations in South Korea, Taiwan, and Hong Kong rapidly declined in the 1960s as living standards and life expectancies increased, just as the fertility of the Japanese population rapidly declined in the 1950s. High population growth rates in the developing world are not the cause of economic stagnation; they are the consequence of it. Indeed, the decline in birth rates following the transition of the economy towards export-oriented labor-intensive manufacturing sets the scene for the transition to more capital-intensive manufacturing half a generation later with the decline in labor force growth that follows a decline in population growth.

The countries in the region—and I include Australia in this observation—do not all realize that South Korea has attained the industrial maturity that Japan attained around 1960 and that Malaysia and Thailand are already at the stage reached reached by South Korea in 1970. Korea experienced real growth in GDP of 12.5 percent in 1978. In that year, the countries of ASEAN also experienced strong growth rates—Thailand 9 percent, Singapore 8.6 percent, Malaysia 7.5 percent, Indonesia 7 percent, the Philippines 5 percent. Hong Kong's growth was 10 percent, Taiwan's 12.8 percent. These figures compare with growth rates of 5.8 percent in Japan, whose economy is leveling off after the rapid expansion of the post-war years, 3.8 percent in the United States, and 2.5 percent in Australia, whose economy is sheltered behind high protectionist barriers and whose government is pursuing deflationary policies in times of record unemployment.[16] By the turn of the century, the Northeast Asian region—China, Taiwan, Korea and Japan—will boast an economy larger than that of Western Europe or North America.

Economic growth in East Asia has generated and been generated by trade in an obviously symbiotic relationship. In 1977, the value of exports of developing East Asian nations, excluding China, was 5.6 times their value in 1970; this figure compares with 3.6 times for the rest of the world.[17] Between 1970 and 1976, direct foreign investment by businessmen of the advanced nations in developing East Asia, excluding China, increased at an annual rate of 21.7 percent.[18] Now one-third of exports from the nations of the East Asia and Australia region, including Japan, are sold to other nations within that region.[19]

Despite the massive levels of American and European ownership of Australian industries, 52 percent of all Australian exports went to East Asia and the Pacific nations in 1977–1978, compared with 29 percent to North American and Europe. This represents a considerable change from 1960–1961, when East Asia and the Pacific took up only 30 percent of exports compared with 52 percent of exports that went to North America and Europe.[20] The importance of East Asia to Australia is irresistibly increasing, while that of North America and, in particular, Europe is irrevocably declining. Between 1972-1973 and 1975-1976, real Australian exports to the ASEAN nations increased at an annual rate of 3.9 percent, those to Japan increased at 1.2 percent per annum, and those to the other developing East Asian market economies—China, Taiwan, Hong Kong, South Korea, and India—at a rate of 12.1 percent per annum. Real exports to the United States, however, declined by 9.2 percent per annum in this period and to the European Community by 12.3 percent per annum. Similarly, over this period, real imports into Australia from the ASEAN countries increased at an annual rate of 15.9 percent, from Japan at an annual rate of 4.3 percent, and from the other East Asian nations at an annual rate of 8.3 percent, compared with an increase of less than 0.3 percent in real imports from the United States and a fall of 4.3 percent in imports from the European Community.[21]

The extent to which Australia has availed herself of the integration of the East Asian economy has been limited by the perspectives of her government. The world has watched as a seemingly endless procession of Australian ministers and officials have addressed arguments, pleas, and protests to the European Community in attempts to secure trade advantages for Australia. Each attempt has met with the resentment and rebuff of the European Community, just as British governments resented and rebuffed Australia's efforts throughout the 1960s to deter Britain from joining the Community. Australia, however, is destined to have an ever-increasing role in the development of East Asia. A Canute and his courtiers cannot hold back this tide.

The position of the United States is a little more ambivalent. She has been surpassed by Japan as the leading investor in the developing East Asian region, just as she has been surpassed by Japan as the major destination for exports. Partly because Japan was a country that imported her technology, but mainly because Japan experienced rapid expansion from being a labor-abundant, Asian economy, most East Asian nations look to Japan as the model for economic growth, rather than to the United States. If we consider the North and West Pacific rim extending from the

United States to Japan to Australia as a region, we find that only 45 percent of American trade is in this region, compared with 57 percent of Japanese trade, 60 percent of Australian trade, 77 percent of Philippine trade, and 84 percent of South Korean trade.[22] While the United States is a vital concern for developing East Asian interests, I think that her economic role is slowly declining, partly due to the booming Japanese economy, partly due to Asian nationalist sentiments, and partly due to the decreasing relevance of American-style foreign investment to the national interests of Asian countries. It is pertinent to note, too, that the developing nations of East Asia and the Pacific will be even less willing—or able—to be involved with the U.S. economy should the multilateral trade negotiations appear to have the effect of a mutual assistance arrangement between the United States, Japan, and Europe.

It is time to look now at China. China has earned more suitors than Turandot. We can only surmise how the libretto and score will end. There can be no doubt that China offers huge trade potential. Prior to the American recognition of Peking, China's Great Leap Outward had already involved her in trade agreements or negotiations with Japan, Britain, the EEC, and the United States. Now that the United States has finally acknowledged the political legitimacy of the government of a quarter of the world's people, the new Chinese leaders and Western capitalists are in a rapturous embrace.

China's plans to mechanize 85 percent of her farm-work process by 1985, compared to the 30 or 40 percent level of mechanization at present, and to increase steel production by 1985 to 2.4 times its present level have been scaled down in the light of reality. Nevertheless, her potential for long-term growth would be hard to overstate. The Chinese have had a particular penchant for "buy back" deals—they are not called "barter" but "buy back"—in which imported technology is repaid in part or full with the goods produced by the use of that technology. While many, if not most, of the goods thus produced may be reserved, initially at least, for domestic consumption, China is laying the foundations for an immense export economy. The immediate prospect for exports is in the traditional areas of clothing and textiles, but her huge population will provide the basis for a whole range of labor-intensive manufactured exports, with obvious great potential for economies of scale in production. China's huge off-shore oil reserves will not be sufficient in themselves to pay for the capital and technology requirements of the Four Modernizations.

China has been the most self-centered, self-satisfied, and self-contained major economy in modern times. She has, however, also created the most socially just society in modern times, eliminating the wretched poverty that characterizes all other developing nations. In the process, she has reduced her population growth rate to 1.2 percent per annum in 1978, and it is hoped it will decline to 0.5 percent by 1985,[23] although, in absolute terms, it is, of course, an enormous problem. Notably, China has succeeded in developing male oral contraception far more quickly than has advanced Western medical technology. Having achieved the goals of her Communist ideology, she now seeks to combine this ideology with capitalist practice to raise the living standards of her population to equal those of the developed world.

For Australia, China offers the opportunity to export particular goods and services, such as agricultural equipment, iron ore, industrial machinery, grain-crops, and technology. The opening of China, however, also portends, for developing East Asian countries as well as for Australia, a possible reduction in the level of foreign investment activity due to the diversion of foreign investment capital to China. In addition, Chinese labor-intensive manufactures and raw materials will be competing in the export markets of East Asian economies. This competition will be fiercest in the area of textiles and, to a lesser degree, electronics. For South Korea and Singapore, where the elementary phases of labor-intensive manufacturing have been superseded, the problems will not be so great. And, indeed, the opportunity to be the gateway for China's freight and tourism will be a significant boost to the Hong Kong economy. For the less developed members of ASEAN, however, particularly Thailand and the Philippines, relying upon growth in textile exports, and Indonesia, relying upon oil and raw material exports, the problems may be great. The success of these economies will depend upon how quickly they will be able to graduate to higher-quality manufactures. For Australia, the reverse is likely to be the case; the opportunities for trade with China should exceed the problems created by the competition China presents in the investment and goods markets.

The enthusiastic participation of China in the regional economy will now give impetus to the idea of a Pacific Community. I first heard of the concept from Takeo Miki in January 1968. Of all the men who have been Prime Ministers of Japan he has not just an unexcelled but an unequaled record as a supporter of democratic institutions. He thought that closer associations between his country and the United States, Canada, Australia, and New Zealand would not only have great economic benefits for all five but would fortify Japan's democratic development and would permit comprehensive initiatives to advance all Pacific countries.

Early in 1973, the new governments of Australia and New Zealand felt that they should help bring about a comprehensive regional organization, without ideological overtones, to help free the Asia Pacific area from great-power intervention and rivalries. I made preliminary and exploratory proposals for such regional cooperation on a visit to Indonesia in February 1973. President Suharto welcomed my objective of a widely representative Asian regional organization and recognized its potential value in the longer term, but he thought that such a concept was unlikely to come about in the short term. There was, at that time, a general feeling among the members of ASEAN that they had to consolidate their own interrelationships before spreading themselves further. Moreover, civil war was still raging in a divided Viet Nam, while China was still ostracized by the United States and in a technical state of war with Japan.

At that time, neither the developed countries of the world nor the developing countries of Southeast Asia realized that the region was so soon to achieve an economic takeoff. The rate of industrial expansion in Britain in the last quarter of the eighteenth century and in the United States in the last quarter of the nineteenth century will be surpassed in East Asia in the last quarter of the twentieth century. This fact was discerned in corporate and academic circles earlier than in political and official circles.

The Pacific Basin Economic Council (PBEC), created by national committees of businessmen in Australia, Canada, Japan, New Zealand, and the United States, held the first of its meetings in Sydney in 1968. I addressed a second meeting in Sydney in 1973. There was a meeting in Los Angeles in May 1979 and in Sydney again in May 1980. PBEC now has a membership of more than 400 major companies. The five national committees have been joined by a Pacific Regional Committee with members from South Korea, Taiwan, Hong Kong, the Philippines, Singapore, Indonesia, Fiji, Mexico, and Peru. It aims to provide an international forum for an exchange of views among businessmen of the Pacific Basin and other nations on topics affecting development of the region and to provide advice and counsel to governments and international agencies on basic economic and business matters affecting the Pacific Basin.

During the same period, Pacific Trade and Development Conferences have been held under academic auspices with Japanese Foreign Office backing. The conferences have tackled many relevant issues and have published many influential papers. The first conference, in Tokyo in January 1968, examined the Pacific free-trade area proposal and alternative trading arrangements. The notion of a free trade area was soon seen to be contrary to the principles espoused by the United States and unattractive to all developing countries. The second conference, in Honolulu in January 1969, considered explicitly the interests and needs of the developing nations of the Pacific. The third conference, held in Sydney in August 1970, was on direct foreign investment in the Pacific region; the fourth, in Ottawa in October 1971, on obstacles to trade in the Pacific area; the fifth, in Tokyo in January 1973, on structural adjustments in Asian-Pacific trade; the sixth, in Mexico City in July 1974, on technology transfer in Pacific economic development; the seventh, in Auckland in August 1975, on relations between large and small countries in the Asia-Pacific region; the eighth, in Thailand in July 1976, on trade and employment; and the ninth in San Francisco in August 1977, on the theme of production, processing, financing, and trade of natural resources in the Pacific Basin. The tenth conference was held in Canberra in March 1979 on ASEAN in the changing Pacific and world economy; the participants were Australia, Canada, Chile, Indonesia, Japan, Malaysia, New Zealand, the Philippines, Singapore, South Korea, Thailand, the United States, and, for the first time, China. An eleventh conference is to be held in Seoul in September 1980.

There has been no corresponding cooperation among trade unions in the region. At an international level, trade union organization is very tenuous. The International Confederation of Free Trade Unions is a less-than-powerful lobby group, while the 16 "international trade secretariats" covering trade union industry groups all have their headquarters in Europe or (in one case) North America.[24] The International Textile, Garment and Leather Workers Federation, for instance, has been so involved with defending the rights of apparel workers in the southern United States that it has been unable to improve the conditions of textile workers in Southeast Asia. Instead, Western trade unions brand the textiles produced in Asia as the products of "sweated labor" and campaign for the imposition of high tariffs on these goods to the detriment of their opposite numbers in Asia.

The establishment of strong regional trade union bodies in the Western Pacific is an inevitability and a necessity for two reasons. Such bodies are the natural and vital way to provide a countervailing force to the internationalization of capital. Such bodies are the only means by which workers in the developed countries in the region will come to appreciate the problems and needs of workers in the developing countries of the region. Governments would be foolish to resist this trend: increasing wages in the region would enhance rather than hinder economic development,[25] and repression of unions and wages would ultimately only lead to political instability in the countries concerned.

The time seems to have come for governments to take a more direct interest in the concept of a Pacific Community which has now had over a decade of support from business and academic circles. Without governments, there can be no satisfactory framework of trade, investment, and communications. For instance, the telecommunication and civil aviation charges in the Pacific are the highest in the world. The General Agreement on Tariffs and Trade (GATT), the International Monetary Fund (IMF), and the U.N. Conference on Trade and Development (UNCTAD) have no specific orientation towards the Pacific or particular interest in it. China, Viet Nam, and Thailand are not members of GATT; the Philippines is only a provisional member; no decision has been made about the membership of Fiji and Papua New Guinea; and Taiwan and Hong Kong are not eligible for membership. China, Viet Nam, and Papua New Guinea are not members of the IMF. Viet Nam and Malaysia are not members of UNCTAD. The OECD is a forum for industrial economies and focuses on Europe rather than on the Pacific. China is not a member of the Asian Development Bank (ADB). It is necessary to consider the basic questions of membership and mechanism of a new and specifically regional body.

No meaningful organization for trade and development in Southeast Asia and the Western Pacific can be created without the participation of ASEAN. All ASEAN's inhibitions seem now to have disappeared. In November 1979, the group inaugurated meetings with Japan at economic ministers' level and made a Cooperation Agreement with the European Community. Japan's full economic attention can scarcely be engaged unless China is also involved. In their visit to Australia and New Zealand in January 1980, Japan's Prime Minister Ohira and his new Foreign Minister Okita, both long-term proponents of the concept, let it be known that any new organization should in principle be open to China and the states of Indochina as well as the Soviet Union. Australia and New Zealand could not decently participate without the membership of the South Pacific Forum, which now comprises all the independent and self-governing states of the South Pacific, all of whom, at this stage, are members of the Commonwealth of Nations. There would seem every reason why both the United States and Canada should become members. Once the United States overcomes her inhibitions about Viet Nam and the super-power blocs recognize both Koreas, there will be a comprehensive membership of the Western Pacific north to south. Moreover, just as Japan's interest in Southeast Asia will facilitate the inclusion of the states of that area, so will United States links with Latin American countries make it likely that ultimately they will join a Pacific organization.

There is not the long history of international cooperation and the sophisticated national structures which would make possible an organization like the OECD. There is not the parity of development and geographic propinquity which have made the European Communities possible. At the present time, there is growing interest in the concept in the U.S. Congress, not least among senators and congressmen from the eastern states. Hugh Patrick, Professor of Far Eastern Economics and Director of the Economic Growth Center at Yale, and Peter Drysdale of the Australian National University have recently prepared a paper for the Senate Foreign Relations Committee's Subcommittee on Asia and the Pacific.[26]

Some of the structures suggested by Patrick and Drysdale are too formal at this stage, while their arguments for U.S. leadership, however necessary to persuade Congress, are too pointed to persuade other countries. A model is at hand in the Commonwealth of Nations, which does not constitute a political bloc but which does hold biennial conferences at which two score heads of government find it useful to exchange views over ten or twelve days. The Commonwealth already embraces many countries in the Pacific: Canada, Australia, New Zealand, the members of the South Pacific Forum, Singapore, and Malaysia. In other parts of the world, the Commonwealth embraces many countries of as great economic and greater ideological diversity. A forum such as the Commonwealth provides would seem to be an effective and acceptable basis for a comprehensive Pacific Community.

It is important to gather accurate and up-to-date information on the national economies within the region. We must concentrate upon improving the standard of information provided by the Asian Development Bank and the Economic and Social Commission for Asia and the Pacific (ESCAP). Ultimately, as anyone familiar with OECD statistics knows, this depends upon the ability of the host countries to collect this sort of data. China collects few statistics and publishes even fewer. (At the plenary meeting of the National People's Congress in June 1979, the Chinese government for the first time released comprehensive statistics on the state of the economy.) Laudable as is the aim of having comprehensive contemporary information, we should hope for, but not expect, miracles to occur in this area.

I have already mentioned the unfavorable conditions under which trade in primary commodities operates, from the point of view of developing nations in the region. Despite the growth of manufactured exports, primary commodities are vital to these economies. It is essential that the iniquitous aspects of the processes of international trade be reformed. The Multilateral Trade Negotiations take two steps backward for one step forward in this regard. Developing countries are justifiably upset that, should the negotiations be ratified, they will be unable to subsidize exports if this reduces the market shares held by developed third-party countries, regardless of whether those market shares were originally carved out by similar export subsidies. It also appears possible that suppliers of raw materials will be unable to restrict exports of such materials in order to build up primary processing industries which, in the long run, may be more efficient than those in the current customer countries. Meanwhile, developed countries will be able to use the "safeguard" clauses of the ensuing agreement to prevent significant increases in access by developing nations to the markets of industrial nations.

Individual commodity agreements, allegedly aimed at preserving the prices of primary commodities exported by developing countries, have been of varying utility. The Lomé Convention, principally involving guaranteed imports by the European Community of sugar produced by 15 developing nations including Fiji and India, resulted in excess sugar being produced by the European Community nations. This sugar was then resold on the world market, further depressing prices of sugar that was not covered by the Convention.[27] Another illustration of the fallibility of commodity agreements is the International Bauxite Association. Australia initiated this association during the term of the Labor Government. Yet, immediately after Australia's present Prime Minister in December 1978 reaffirmed in Jamaica his support for the developing nations' quest for unified commodity agreements, his Deputy Prime Minister announced that Australia was to repudiate her undertakings to the association and undercut the other member nations.

An integrated program for commodities—not just single-commodity agreements—is essential for the amelioration of the grievances of developing countries. It is most pleasing that agreement has finally been reached on the establishment of a Common Fund. Its efficacy will now depend upon the willingness of Western governments to finance its operations and upon the motivation of the people chosen to administer it. The most recent session of the United Nations Conference on Trade and Development (UNCTAD V) in May 1979, however, saw little progress in raising finance for the Common Fund. The expected size of the First Window of the Fund, through which buffer stocks are to be financed, is only one-twelfth of that originally proposed. No formula has yet been agreed to regarding subscriptions and few countries have pledged contributions. The spirit of the Second Window, aimed in part at encouragement of new industries in developing countries, is contradicted by the Multilateral Trade Negotiations (mentioned above).

As great a problem, at least for the more advanced developing nations in East Asia, is the protectionist barriers facing their exports to Europe, Australia, and North America. In each case, employers and unions find common cause in pressuring politicians to erect those barriers. Their representations and defeatism involve a risk to the trade of the developed nations themselves. Tariffs added to exports of developing nations are, on average, 50 percent higher than tariffs added to exports of developed countries.[28] These tariffs discriminate particularly against the manufactured products of developing nations. ASEAN has been overt in its criticism of Australia, which it sees as viewing ASEAN and developing countries generally "only as a source of supply of certain basic raw materials for her industrial inputs" while "processed and manufactured products are often classified as threats to her high cost industries and extremely high tariffs intended to protect local industries are imposed on finished products."[29] Japan and North America fare no better in ASEAN eyes. Import quotas and ceilings, discretionary licensing, variable levies, and a plethora of other devices serve to impede the manufactured exports and economic growth of developing East Asian nations. These nations, before long, will make their attitudes on protectionism known to the developed countries of Western Europe and North America as they already have to Australia.

The countries that have succeeded best in developing industrial manufacturing sectors are those that have succeeded best in improving nutrition, life expectancy, infant survival, and literacy. Amongst the 24 developing member countries of the Asian Development Bank, the 4 most industrialized nations—South Korea, Hong Kong, Taiwan, and Singapore—rank first, second, third, and fourth in terms of life expectancy; second, third, fourth, and tenth in terms of infant survival; first, second, third, and fifth in terms of average protein intake; second, third, fourth, and fifth in terms of high school enrolment ratios; and second, third, sixth, and eighth in terms of literacy rates.[30] It is important to note that, in South Korea and Taiwan, land reform and heavy investment in education preceded and accompanied economic growth. If, however, the developed nations of the region continue to erect barriers to trade and perpetuate a process by which the conditions of trade disadvantage the developing nations of the region, then we shall see obstructions on the paths to development towards a more equitable distribution of the region's and the world's wealth and resources, towards regional mutuality and towards the economic growth of an area that may well provide the stimulus that the developed world needs. Again, progress at UNCTAD V was very limited in this area. While all nations publicly condemned protectionism, none of the developed countries were willing to pledge reductions in protection afforded their own domestic industries.

Too many articles and lectures on the Western Pacific have dwelt on the effects that actions and ideologies and strategies elsewhere will have on the region. Governments are now realizing, as transnational corporations and learned institutions have already realized, that there now exist a clear Western Pacific economic identity and community that are growing in strength. The governments of the developed nations of Western Europe and North America have a legacy of political involvement in the Western Pacific which has often made them slow to discern the nature and degree of the region's economic development. Western European and now American banks and financial institutions and transnational corporations have had fewer inhibitions about this development. The U.S. economy has tilted towards the western states, which are acquiring the space and computer industries of the future. The world's economy is shifting its center of gravity from the mid-Atlantic to the mid-Pacific. By the year 2000, the East Asian economy will be as large as the North American or Western European or Eastern European. Western prosperity will be greatly affected by Western readiness, governmental and corporate, to recognize economic developments and requirements in the Western Pacific, the most dynamic region in the world.

THREE

Politics of the Western Pacific

Viet Nam's victory in her war of independence was the denouement of the effort by the United States, with one significant ally, Australia, throughout the 1950s and 1960s to control the politics of the Western Pacific by isolating and boycotting China. The first act in this strategy had been the severance of Taiwan from China and the division of China's neighbors, Korea and Viet Nam. The scenario was developed in the context of encompassing the globe with military pacts. When the Stars and Stripes replaced the Tricolor in Viet Nam, Dulles devised the South-East Asian Collective Defense Treaty (SEATO), composed of the United States, the United Kingdom, France, Australia, New Zealand, Pakistan, and two nations in Southeast Asia, the Philippines and Thailand. At high noon in Viet Nam, President Johnson sponsored the Asian and Pacific Council (ASPAC) so as to corral Taiwan and those Asian nations that recognized Taipei as the capital of China— South Korea, Japan, South Viet Nam, Thailand, Malaysia, the Philippines, Australia, and New Zealand. I recite this sustained history of divisive and misplaced ingenuity in order to highlight the stunning and sudden political transformation in the 1970s. Where are the pacts of yesteryear?

Since so much treasure and so many lives were dissipated in pursuing political objectives in the Western Pacific, especially Viet Nam, an initial fact we must face is that Americans have not been

engaged in hostilities in that part or in any part of the world under
the terms of any military pact. U.S. forces were not involved in
hostilities in West or East Malaysia, as Australian forces were. In
the early 1960s during Indonesia's *confrontasi*, Secretary Rusk
gave an assurance that Australian ships in the Borneo area would
be covered by the Security Treaty (Australia, New Zealand, United States)—ANZUS—the pact which the United States entered
into in order to reconcile Australians and New Zealanders to the
Japan peace treaty and to help the reelection of the Menzies
Government in Australia in 1951. President Kennedy soon after
declared that Secretary Rusk had exceeded his authority in giving
such an assurance. Similarly, United States intervention in Indochina did not take place under SEATO.

The evasions and misrepresentations of political leaders concerning the U.S. role in Viet Nam and Cambodia were not con-
fined to the United States. The first necessity in framing a policy
in relation to the Western Pacific is to learn from the mistakes in
the recent past and to restore our political credibility. I shall
illustrate from the conduct of Australian political leaders. When
the Australian Minister for Defence in February 1965 raised the
possibility of a SEATO operation in Viet Nam, Mr. William
Bundy, the U.S. Assistant Secretary of State for Far Eastern
Affairs, pointed out that, for SEATO to operate, South Viet Nam
would have to appeal for help and he doubted that this was wise
for fear of refusal by some members. In March 1965, there were
crucial military staff talks between Australia and the United States
in Honolulu concerning the provision of military aid to Viet Nam.
Australia told Britain that they were informal talks arising out of
ANZUS affairs. This was deceitful conduct: Britain, being still a
co-chairman of the Geneva Conference on Viet Nam, was entitled
to be told the truth. No suggestion was made by either the United
States or Australia that these crucial talks, as a result of which
Australian combat troops were committed to Viet Nam, were in
any way part of a SEATO operation. Australian military aid to
South Viet Nam was, in fact, offered and supplied in response to
the known and frequently expressed wishes of the United States

for political support from her friends and allies. The U.S. Administration desired the military presence of her friends and allies in order to prove to the world and her own electorate that the United States was not alone in her efforts against communism in Southeast Asia, in order to show that she was not replicating French colonialism in the area, and in order to reassure governments indigenous to the area that members of SEATO were, in fact, prepared to make a practical contribution to defenses against communism. The government of South Viet Nam, on 29 April 1965, announced that the Australian battalion was sent in response to a request from South Viet Nam; but this is not borne out by the evidence of the documents.[1] Australian military assistance to South Viet Nam was not at any time given in response to a request for defense aid from South Viet Nam as a Protocol State to SEATO as a treaty organization. Although successive Australian governments sought publicly to justify their actions as being "in the context of" or "flowing from" Australia's membership in SEATO and the theory of the Protocol State, or on the ground that military assistance under SEATO could be on a bilateral as well as a collective basis, the commitment was, in fact, not made under SEATO.

Before combat troops were committed by Australia in 1965 to South Viet Nam, some military instructors were sent on two occasions. On 24 May 1962, the Minister for Defence announced publicly that Australia was providing these instructors "at the invitation of the government of the Republic of Viet Nam." That statement has no factual basis evident in the documents. On 9 June 1964, the Minister for Defence announced that Australia would be sending some additional army instructors. The decision and the announcement were made before the government of South Viet Nam was consulted or informed.

The significant commitment, that of combat troops, was made in April 1965. The documents show quite clearly that they were not sent as part of, or in response to, SEATO Council planning; nor were they sent in response to an appeal to SEATO as a collective organization from South Viet Nam as a Protocol State of

SEATO. There is no evidence in official documents that the South Vietnamese government had made any request for the first increase in Australian troop levels which was announced on 18 August 1965. Nor is there any firm evidence to suggest that the Vietnamese were consulted. A second increase was announced on 8 March 1966; in that case the Australian Ambassador in Saigon was informed of the decision on 4 March and instructed to work out with the Vietnamese government the terms of a letter of request. A third increase was announced on 20 December 1966; there is no documentary evidence that the government of the Republic of Viet Nam was consulted about it or given prior notification of it. The fourth and final increase was announced on 17 October 1967, after extremely strong pressure from the President of the United States but without any request from Viet Nam.

After their immense efforts, often misguided and even misleading, to control political developments in the Western Pacific in the 1960s, political leaders in the United States and in Australia now show a disposition to give too little attention to political developments. I have stressed the resources and trade of the region as of primary importance. This is not to say, however, that there are not still political issues that should have our attention. Some will not diminish, still less disappear, through inattention, and some new issues may arise.

In the last four years, there has been a great change in the condition of those three East Asian states whose division the United States procured or welcomed at the end of the 1940s and the beginning of the 1950s. Viet Nam is now united, as one assumes that her people always desired. There was no cultural or historical basis for believing that Viet Nam should be divided. There had been no division for at least a thousand years.

China is recognized as one country. It is true that it was possible—it came as a rush at the end of 1972—for other nations to have diplomatic representatives in both South and North Viet Nam, in both South and North Korea, in both East and West Germany. It was never possible, however, for any nation to have diplomatic representatives in both Peking and Taipei. Whatever faults the government in Peking attributed to the late Generalissimo Chiang Kai-shek, the members of that government always, in my experience, paid tribute to him as a patriot in one respect: he always asserted that there was one China and he always asserted that Taiwan was a province of China. He claimed to be the leader of a government that was the sole legitimate government of the whole of China, of which Taiwan was one of the provinces. If any nation had, at any time in the 1950s or 1960s, sought to send a diplomatic representative accredited to Chiang Kai-shek as President of Taiwan, the credentials of that representative would have been rejected. Tremendous ingenuity has been misplaced over three decades in suggesting that there could be a two-China policy. There never could be, because neither of the rival governments themselves would accept it.

There is still a third divided country in the Western Pacific — Korea. The basic situation in Korea is that, as far back in history as one can explore, Korea has been united. More so than Viet Nam, she is and has been ethnically and culturally homogeneous. There is no justification for having two Koreas. One would think that the only persons who stand to benefit from the present division are the leaders of the two competing and extremist regimes and their supporting elites; one would think they would be a minority in both halves of the country.

This is not to say that, in 1950 and in the last 1940s, the United States was not avid to see Korea divided. I presume the same opinion was held in the Soviet Union, because both countries combined to divide Korea. The division was imposed from outside. It is to be doubted if either country had clean hands over the outbreak of war in Korea in 1950. Less than a week before war erupted, before the United Nations authorized military action, the Australian government had received reports of intended South Korean aggressions from its representative in South Korea. The evidence was sufficiently strong for the Australian Prime Minister to authorize a cable to Washington urging that no encouragement be given to the South Korean government. The cable cannot now be found among official papers in Australia; perhaps it will turn up in Washington under the Freedom of Information Act.

What interest does the United States now have in Korea's being divided still? I am disappointed that there is so little public debate on this issue. Any United States administration has immense and innumerable problems to tackle. It needs the support of an alert and informed public. The present administration, if I may venture to say so, has taken action on a great number of fronts on which previous U.S. administrations, Democratic and Republican, have too long hesitated to take action. The present administration has acted on Panama. The present administration has acted on China. The present administration is willing to act on Southern Africa. The present administration has taken some action in Western Asia, that is, the Middle East, although it is generally acknowledged that there can be no peace between Israel and the Arab states other than Egypt, and that there can be no peace within Israel or the neighboring Arab states until there is a homeland for the Palestinians; it is also generally acknowledged that there will be terrorism in Israel by the P.L.O. and by Israeli forces against Lebanon, which is too weak to hit back, until there is a homeland for the Palestinians. If successive Presidents had been perceived to be doing more to persuade Israel to heed the repeated and overwhelming U.N. calls to evacuate Palestinian territories, the United States would have met with more enthusiasm in the Middle East and the Moslem world for her efforts to persuade the Soviet Union to heed the overwhelming United Nations call to evacuate Afghanistan. (One might note the inevitable growth of support for the Palestinian cause in ASEAN.) The present administration also has shown some disposition to tackle the Korean question.

Not even, however, in the United States, possibly least of all in the United States, should the public be content to wait until an administration moves. I notice some tendency within the American media to blame this administration for not anticipating various events in other continents and not alerting the public to them. Surely the media and the various experts did not have to rely on successive administrations for information on South Viet

Nam. Surely they could have ascertained the presence of Cubans in Angola; they had been there for quite some years before they came into conflict with one of the factions supported by a U.S. agency and the South Africans. More recently, the administration has been criticized for not discerning the erosion of the authority of the Shah of Iran in the most remarkable revolution in sweep and speed in modern history. Surely the resources of a powerful press were adequate to make an independent assessment. At least, the administration and the media between them have not been able to discover that the Russians were to blame for either restoring or overthrowing the Shah.

It should be possible for people outside the administration to help create a climate for reassessing the division of Korea, for discussing the basic issue: Why is Korea divided? One thing at least is clear: it was not divided by the Koreans. If this is so, what advantage is there to the United States in Korea's being divided today? I would not think that the United States or the U.S.S.R., which incidentally has left North Korea with definitely second-rate equipment, would see any advantage in allowing a war between North and South Korea. I would not think that China would see any advantage in having a war between North and South Korea. Nevertheless, Korea represents a part of the world with a great potential for drawing the superpowers into conflict.

At present, a rather delicate balance of power exists around the peninsula between moderate regimes in each of China, the U.S.S.R., Japan, and the United States. None of them is as bellicose as both North and South Korea have been. We must acknowledge the possibility that either North or South Korea might see some advantage in having hostilities with the other. This small possibility will increase in likelihood if one half becomes a major economic or military power without the other half enjoying similar development. The rapid growth of South Korea portends that this may occur. We must further acknowledge that it would be possible for the United States to be involved against her wishes. One only has to look at the situation where countries that depend on a U.S. guarantee, such as Israel, are quite ready to ignore U.S.

wishes. Settlements proceed on the West Bank of the Jordan. The U.S. Administration does not approve of them, but they go ahead. What would be the situation if there were an actual war between North and South Korea, as far as relations between China and the United States are concerned? It would be the only issue I can imagine on which there would be any incentive for the Soviet Union and China to see eye to eye. It would be difficult for either of them to abandon North Korea and leave the other to support North Korea alone.

I would urge these propositions upon public opinion in the United States: (1) To seek cross-recognition of the two Koreas by the big powers. (The assassination of President Park on 26 October 1979 showed how advantageous it would have been for the United States to have representatives in Pyongyang as well as Seoul. She could have secured more direct information and she could have offered more direct advice.) (2) To support admission of both Koreas to the United Nations. Both courses have been followed in relation to the two Germanies. If one cannot bring about unification, one can at least facilitate coexistence. Certainly the same arguments ought to be urged in the Soviet Union and China and Japan.

Before 1962, no country recognized both the Republic of Korea and the Democratic People's Republic of Korea. In that year, Egypt, which had recognized the ROK in 1961, also extended recognition to the DPRK. Egypt's initiative was followed by another country in 1964, 2 others in 1969, another in 1970 and 2 others in 1971. Recognition of the two Koreas gained momentum in 1972 when 10 countries which had previously recognized only the ROK also extended recognition to the DPRK. In 1973, 10 more did so; in 1974, 11 (including Australia); and in 1975, 2. Of the countries which had hitherto recognized the DPRK alone, 1 also recognized the ROK in 1973, another in 1974, a third in 1977, 3 more in 1978, and 1 in 1979. Both the ROK and DPRK were recognized simultaneously by 3 countries in 1973, by 1 in 1974, and by 2 in 1975, 1976, and 1977. Only the Warsaw and NATO powers have remained stiff-necked on this issue, except that Norway, disagreeing with her NATO allies, joined the other

Nordics in completing their recognition of both the ROK and DPRK in mid-1973. In the Western Pacific, there are many countries that have diplomatic relations with both North and South. There are 96 nations in the world that recognize North Korea and 113 that recognize South Korea; there are 57, more than half of those in each of the two categories, that accord diplomatic recognition to both. Four of the 5 ASEAN nations recognize both, the Philippines being the exception. All the countries on the Indian subcontinent recognize both: India, Pakistan, Bangladesh, Sri Lanka, Burma, and Nepal. In the South Pacific, Australia, Papua New Guinea, Fiji, and Western Samoa recognize both.

In the light of China's invasion of Viet Nam subsequent to but not solely consequent on Viet Nam's intervention in Kampuchea, it is ironic to recall what was said in the 1950s and 1960s to justify the division of Viet Nam and America's military intervention in the South and assaults on the North. Here again I shall cite Australians. In April 1965, Australia's initial military commitment in South Viet Nam was justified in the flamboyant and fantastic words of the Australian Prime Minister as designed to thwart "the downward thrust of Communist China between the Indian and Pacific Oceans." The leader on the other side of Australian politics had earlier expressed alarm at the red lava flowing down over Viet Nam.

My public speeches on Viet Nam in the United States were made at the National Press Club in Washington, the first in July 1973 and the second in May 1975. "For 20 years," I said on the earlier occasion, "I have been appalled at the damage we of the West have done to ourselves and to other peoples by our Western ideological preoccupations, particularly in Southeast Asia. We are not going to be readily forgiven for throwing away the chance we had for a settlement in Indochina in 1954, after Korea, after Geneva." On the second occasion, nearly five years ago, I said: "Are we to treat Viet Nam after 1975 as we treated China after 1949? Through fear or frustration, because of our failure to impose the will of the West on Indochina, are we to treat Viet Nam as the new pariah, the new untouchable among nations? No one supposes that it is going to be a simple or easy task to establish meaningful relations with Viet Nam, a Viet Nam emerging from thirty years of civil war prolonged and deepened by foreign intervention. It is going to be one of the most difficult tasks for statesmanship, for countries in Australia's region and for the United States.

"Two hundred years ago, on 22 March 1777, Edmund Burke said 'Magnanimity in politics is not seldom the truest wisdom.' It was in his great speech on conciliation with the American colonies. He was advising another mighty nation which was about to suffer humiliation at the hands of another small band of revolutionaries—not because that nation was wicked or weak, but because it was committed to policies doomed to fail. Magnanimity in the face of failure is much more difficult than magnanimity in victory. The present prosperity of West Germany and Japan attest America's unparalleled magnanimity in victory. The other, more difficult, response lies ahead—in Indochina.

"In the specific matter of Viet Nam, I am not going to be panicked by an outcome achieved militarily in 1975 which might have come about politically in 1954. I am intent upon reaching a modus vivendi, a meaningful and constructive relationship with Viet Nam in 1975, as we would assuredly have had to do sometime between 1954 and 1975, and as, with such needless and damaging delay, we have done with China."

Just as the United States failed to face facts by normalizing relations with Communist China at the outset and then found in the Korean War an excuse for not doing so, so now the United States is using the invasion of Kampuchea as an excuse for not normalizing relations with Viet Nam as she should have done years earlier. It is true that the United States did not persist in blocking the admission of Viet Nam to the United Nations for as many years as she persisted in blocking the admission of China. Nevertheless, she still refuses to establish diplomatic relations with Viet Nam. Those of her NATO allies who still go along with her ostracism of North Korea do not support her ostracism of Viet Nam. Diplomatic relations have been established between

Viet Nam and 99 other nations. Among them are all America's NATO allies, all (now that Ireland has established diplomatic relations with Viet Nam) the OECD countries. America's political boycott has no support and will get none. It is one of those issues that is not going to disappear or even diminish through inattention.

I cannot forget the account Adlai Stevenson gave me in July 1964 of why and how President Kennedy had failed to reassess America's policy on China. During his election campaign, Kennedy had been briefed by Eisenhower and supported by Henry Luce on condition that he not abandon Taiwan. The most Kennedy would allow Stevenson to do as U.S. Representative to the United Nations was to cease the U.S. opposition in committee to inscribing the China question on the agenda of the General Assembly. Stevenson was instructed, however, to frustrate any change in the Assembly itself. He had to adopt the device of securing a resolution that any proposal to change the representation of China was an important question under Article 18 of the Charter of the United Nations and therefore required a two-thirds majority of the members present and voting. The President wanted no actions that would impede him in securing a better majority when he stood for reelection.

I have often thought how much travail the United States would have been spared if, at that time, she had abandoned the myths about China that were used to justify the war in Viet Nam. The charade continued for many years after Ambassador Stevenson's own death. Finally, in October 1971, the General Assembly decided by more than a two-thirds majority to recognize the People's Republic of China and to expel the representatives of Chiang Kai-shek. It took another seven years for the United States to accept the situation. How much longer will it take the United States to reassess her Viet Nam policy?

The fact that Viet Nam now appears to be excessively in the Soviet Union's pocket is the fault of the West. Among the developed nations, Sweden has been the only consistent, generous provider of assistance over the years. The United States' official development assistance has been niggardly in Southeast Asia, as everywhere else; Japan's is worse. The United States has not only refused to establish diplomatic relations with Viet Nam but has embargoed trade with Viet Nam and has subverted the Articles of the World Bank and the Asian Development Bank (ADB) to prevent them from granting assistance to Viet Nam. These are strong words but words that can be justified.

Most assistance to developing countries has come through the soft windows of the World Bank and the ADB. Three years ago, Viet Nam joined both banks. She clearly qualifies for assistance from them. She has not received it.

The soft window of the World Bank—the International Development Association (IDA)—stems from a plan put forward by former Senator Monroney of Oklahoma. By January 1960, the Executive Directors of the Bank had drawn up articles of agreement of the IDA. Under Article I, "The purposes of the Association are to promote economic development, increase productivity, and thus raise standards of living in the less-developed areas of the world included within the Association's membership . . ." Under Article V, Section 6, "The Association and its officers shall not interfere in the political affairs of any member; nor shall they be influenced in their decisions by the political character of the member or members concerned. Only economic considerations shall be relevant to their decisions, and these considerations shall be weighed impartially in order to achieve the purposes stated in this Agreement."

The Asian Development Bank stems from President L.B. Johnson's proposals for a Marshall Plan for Asia. Under the sponsorship of the Economic Commission for Asia and the Far East (ECAFE), now the Economic and Social Commission for Asia and the Pacific (ESCAP), articles were drawn up in Manila in December 1965. Under Article 1, "The purpose of the Bank shall be to foster economic growth and cooperation in the region of Asia and the Far East and to contribute to the acceleration of the process of economic development of the developing countries in the region, collectively and individually." Under Article 2 (ii),

"The Bank shall have the function to utilize the resources at its disposal for financing development of the developing member countries in the region, giving priority to those regional, sub-regional as well as national projects and programmes which will contribute most effectively to the harmonious economic growth of the region as a whole, and having special regard to the needs of the smaller or less developed member countries in the region." Under Article 36,

1. The Bank shall not accept loans or assistance that may in any way prejudice, limit, deflect or otherwise alter its purpose or functions; and

2. The Bank, its President, Vice-President(s), officers and staff shall not interfere in the political affairs of any member, nor shall they be influenced in their decisions by the political character of the member concerned. Only economic considerations shall be relevant to their decisions. Such considerations shall be weighed impartially in order to achieve and carry out the purpose and functions of the Bank.

On 2 July 1976, the Republic of South Viet-Nam, which replaced the Republic of Viet-Nam, and the Democratic Republic of Viet-Nam united to constitute the Socialist Republic of Viet Nam. On 21 September 1976, with the U.S. Executive Director alone voting against it, the SRVN joined the World Bank, the first Communist state to do so since Yugoslavia and Romania. An introductory economic report by the Bank on 12 August 1977 stated, Viet Nam's "natural assets combined with a literate and well-organized population give the country a considerable development potential." The International Monetary Fund, in a report of 14 October 1977 on recent economic developments, stated "The long-run economic prospects appear favorable. Viet Nam is rich in natural resources and has a disciplined and educated labor force." In 1978, the Bank approved a $60-million credit for an irrigation project in the southwest. In its 1979 annual report, the Bank stated, "Some 21,000 farm families or about 110,000 people will benefit . . . About 30,000 seasonal jobs will be created during the construction period. The Kuwait Fund for Arab Economic Development and the OPEC Special Fund, as well as the

Netherlands, are helping co-finance the project, with loans of $10 million each." The United States deducted its $20 million share.

In October 1976, the SRVN took over ADB membership of the former RSV-N and accepted responsibility for all of the outstanding obligations to the Bank in respect of the previous loans to the former government. Early in 1978, the SRVN agreed to take responsibility for the Japanese loans to the defunct Saigon regime. In 1978, the ADB reactivated 6 loans covering 5 projects. The ADB, however, has not made any new loan to Viet Nam since 1975. The Directors have denied funds for new projects to Viet Nam alone among the Bank's 21 borrowers. The only new project administered by the Bank was financed by the OPEC Special Fund. This was a project for modernizing 600 fishing vessels and rehabilitating 4,600 others as part of Viet Nam's Five-Year (1976–1980) Development Plan. The Bank noted the very high rates of return, the increased employment, income, and living standards, and the substantial export income the project would provide and considered "the substantial developmental and financial requirements of post-war Viet Nam." Several requests, equally worthy, have been made for assistance from the ADB's own funds and are at different stages of processing. The staff of the Bank have made a number of inspections in Viet Nam but have not thought it prudent to advance any proposals to their Board for consideration. This has been due to the heavy-handedness and vindictiveness of the U.S. House of Representatives. In 1977 and 1978, the House passed amendments to the Foreign Assistance appropriations precluding the use of U.S. funds for Viet Nam, Laos, Kampuchea, Angola, and the Central African Empire. The articles of the World Bank and the Asian Development Bank, which I have quoted, prohibit them from accepting funds with such political restrictions. The agreements establishing their soft windows require every donor to meet its share of replenishment funds; the default by any donor puts an end to the obligations of all the other donors. The denial of U.S. funds would, thus, force both banks to stop their development operations immediately. The amendments were not persevered with after President Carter wrote to the House Committee that the U.S. director of each bank would oppose any loans to Viet Nam and the other outcasts.

On 6 September 1979, the House again amended the Foreign Assistance appropriation for the financial year 1980. On 2 October 1979, Mr. Robert McNamara told the World Bank meeting in Belgrade: "The blunt truth is that, if this amendment is finally enacted into law, the House will literally have destroyed the largest single source of economic assistance to the one and a quarter billion people living in the poorest developing countries." On 12 October, the Senate passed the appropriation without amendment. Conferences between the Houses on 31 October and 1 November failed to resolve their differences. On 1 November, McNamara wrote to the Chairman of the House Subcommittee on Foreign Operations:

> In response to your inquiry, I would like you to know that events over the past year have raised a very serious question about Viet Nam's current commitment to a rational development policy. These questions were considered sufficiently fundamental to warrant a suspension of new lending to Viet Nam.
>
> Under current conditions it would not be possible to invest funds there with a high probability that investment objectives would be realized or with assurances that the project would benefit the masses of the people. Consequently, because of these conditions, I cannot recommend a loan to Viet Nam to the Board in FY1980 and therefore the Bank Group will not be providing a loan to Viet Nam in FY1980.

McNamara's capitulation and a corresponding letter from the U.S. Treasury conveying similar advice from the U.S. Executive Director of the ADB were to no avail because the Congress rose for Christmas without making an appropriation for FY 1980. Foreign aid funding will continue at the fiscal 1979 level or at the House-passed level for fiscal 1980, whichever is the lower, and the United States will retain her reputation as a defaulter with international institutions.

Viet Nam, by joining the World Bank and ADB and taking over South Viet Nam's commitments, had shown her anxiety to be accepted as part of the world economic community and not to be isolated in the Chinese or Soviet economic blocs. Her dire economic needs and Western indifference to them have driven her closer to the Soviet Union. The fewer friends one has, the closer one gets to them.

In June 1978, the Australian Ambassador to Viet Nam was upset when, along the long, long way to Hanoi's international airport, we were hailed as "Russians." It was almost a flashback to ten years earlier, when all Caucasians on the way to Saigon's airport were greeted as "Americans."

Economic sanctions against Viet Nam are unlikely to succeed. Viet Nam is more likely than any other country in Southeast Asia to have the same system of government in the year 2000 as she has today. Her leaders have shown astonishing solidarity and stamina. They are experienced and unyielding. President Ton Duc Thang, Ho Chi Minh's successor, went to France and joined her navy in 1912. He sailed into Sydney before World War I. His revolutionary activities go back at least to November 1917, when he celebrated the Russian Revolution by raising the red flag on his ship in Odessa. He died on 30 March 1980 at the age of 91.

America's longstanding trade and aid boycott against Viet Nam is now said to be justified by the border and refugee disputes which came to a head in 1979. Disputes on both issues demonstrated the consequences of international inaction and indifference.

Newly independent states are all willing to go to war to fight for the borders they inherited from their old imperial masters. They are as stubborn as the oldest states in asserting the sanctity of existing borders. The resolution of border disputes is an intractable problem. No state is prepared to sponsor a process for realigning borders. Such a principle would lead to the break-up of such large entities as the U.S.S.R., China, and India, which all claim to be multinational states, while the United States herself knows that she might be vulnerable to Hispanic separatism by the end of this century. New Mexico could revert to Mexico. Border disputes will not disappear or diminish through inattention. They need working on. There are border disputes between Viet Nam and Kampuchea but also between Thailand and Kampuchea; there have been for centuries. Every ASEAN country except Singapore has an historical claim to some of the territory of another ASEAN country; and Singapore would like some more islands. Growing cooperation within ASEAN has diminished such issues amongst its members.

In February 1978, Viet Nam made a three-point proposal to settle all problems concerning the relations between her and Kampuchea, the third point suggesting agreement on an appropriate form of international guarantee and supervision. The offer was forwarded to the Secretary-General of the United Nations and to the Coordinating Bureau of the Non-Aligned Countries. None of the neighbors responded; nor did Australia. The Pol Pot government aroused no international reaction with its constant forays into Viet Nam during the rest of the year; the Vietnamese government retaliated after Christmas, and at last there was international reaction.

Her neighbors and the United States show most interest in Viet Nam on the subject of refugees. First, Viet Nam sent troops into Kampuchea in order to remove a government from which refugees were fleeing into Viet Nam. Next, China invaded northern Viet Nam in order to punish a government from which refugees were fleeing into China.

In Geneva, in May 1978, it was brought to my notice by the U.N. High Commissioner for Refugees and by the International Committee of the Red Cross that the country in the region with the greatest number of refugees was Viet Nam—150,000. By the end of 1978, this number had doubled, while 240,000 from Viet Nam had taken refuge in the two neighboring provinces of China. None of the countries in Southeast Asia or indeed in the rest of the world seemed to be much agitated about the refugees in Viet Nam and China, nor about 40,000 who went from East to West Timor in 1975 and 200,000 from Burma into Bangladesh in 1978 and the 90,000 refugees from Mindanao to Sabah. It is about the untold thousands of refugees who have left Viet Nam by sea for Malaysia, Indonesia, Australia, Hong Kong, and the Philippines that there has been so much international concern.

The Western media, for over twenty years, have been accustomed to condemn the Communist governments of Russia and East Germany for impeding the departure of their citizens. They are nonplused when the Communist government of Viet Nam, which has also been consistently condemned, not only allows its unwilling and unwelcome citizens to depart but in fact seems to encourage them to do so. It is ironic that so many critics of Russia and East Germany now appear to urge Viet Nam to adopt the policies they have condemned on the part of Russia and East Germany. It is irrelevant to the present situation that Viet Nam has a Communist government. Older and larger refugee problems have been caused by governments in Western Asia, but Turkish, Israeli, and Lebanese leaders cannot be classified as Communists. Refugees would not have gone from Kampuchea into Viet Nam and from Viet Nam into China in 1977 and 1978 if their main motive was to escape from a Communist government.

The tide of refugees has reached its present proportions for economic and ethnic reasons. Insofar as the present exodus from Viet Nam is due to economic conditions, it will be exacerbated by the refusal of some countries to extend or continue economic aid to that country. Insofar as the exodus from Viet Nam is due to racial tensions, it will be exacerbated by the continuation or escalation of tension between China and that country. It is probable that hundreds of thousands of residents of Viet Nam still wish to leave the country, even if the government takes no action to speed their departure. Those who constantly proclaim the imminence of invasion must bear much of the responsibility for people fleeing from their homes and even their homelands.

The United Nations has drawn up four conventions on refugees: the 1951 Convention and 1967 Protocol relating to the Status of Refugees; the 1954 Convention relating to the Status of Stateless Persons; and the 1961 Convention on the Reduction of Statelessness. Australia is the only country in Southeast Asia that has ratified them, although it took her twenty years to withdraw her last reservation to the first, and she did not ratify the others till 1973 and 1974 respectively. None of the conventions has been applied to Hong Kong or ratified by China, Japan, Viet Nam, India, Pakistan, or any of the ASEAN countries. The United States has ratified only the 1967 Protocol. At the meeting on refugees and displaced persons in Southeast Asia, attended by 57 countries in Geneva on 20 and 21 July 1979, it was found that the only countries, apart from Australia, that had ratified all four conventions were Britain and Ireland, Denmark, Norway, Sweden, West Germany, and Costa Rica. On 30 May 1979, Viet Nam and the UNHCR agreed on arrangements for the departure of persons from Viet Nam. The arrangements are working well. In October, the UNHCR reopened the office in Ho Chi Minh City, which had closed in April 1975. In November it opened an office in Peking, the PRC having taken up Taiwan's place in June 1979. If orderly and humane arrangements are to be made for refugees to secure homes and status, then affected or interested countries must at least ratify the conventions that are already available and conclude further conventions as circumstances dictate.

The situation of the boat people of Vietnamese stock may be likened to that of the Cubans who, in numbers exceeding 600,000, have left their country under an agreement whereby exit visas from Cuba are matched with entry visas from countries offering permanent settlement. The situation of the boat people of Chinese stock has some parallel with that of the Indians in East Africa and the British in Southern Africa. While these Chinese, Indians, and British may be an ethnic minority in the countries they leave, they belong to the ethnic majority in several other countries. The ancestors of these Chinese, Indians, and British, sometimes two or three generations back, came to their present countries of residence during the heyday of British and French imperial expansion. Not all would wish to go back to their ethnic homelands in China, India, and Britain. One would expect that China, a country with the largest population and one of the largest areas in the world, will be the ultimate destination of many *hua* people from Viet Nam. Many of the capitalist *hua* people, however, would prefer to go to Singapore or Taiwan; it is hard to justify the refusal to let them land in either place.

It is sheer realism to acknowledge that the governments of Malaysia and Indonesia are reluctant to have an increase in their Chinese populations. Those ethnic Chinese whom China has not yet taken and whom Singapore and Taiwan will not take will have to be accommodated elsewhere, and clearly most of them will have to be accommodated outside the immediate region. The reception of the boat people has already caused disputes amongst some of the ASEAN countries; it can cause disputes between Australia and some of them.

It is foolish to assert that it is easier for the boat people to settle in Australia than in other countries in the region. Australians have never taken the trouble to explain that most of their country is uninhabitable. The refugees heading south are city dwellers. One of the reasons they wish to leave southern Viet Nam is the pressure on them to live in the new zones in the countryside. Like 80 percent of Australia's immigrants, they will come to live in Sydney and Melbourne, which are as crowded as the city state of Singapore, which repulses refugees, and the British colony of Hong Kong, which has taken 67,000 boat people and up to 23,000 legal and illegal immigrants by land. ASEAN and Australia cannot be expected to solve the problem of the boat people by themselves. The problem is going to challenge the world for many years.

The refugee situation has shown that it can be a threat to peace in East Asia. The aim must be to relieve Viet Nam of her dependency and isolation. There is every reason to assume that this follows the wishes of the Vietnamese themselves, for they have fought long and hard to assert their independence from French colonizers and American intruders and have no innate propensity to discard the results of these struggles and become subservient to the Soviet Union.

It is always possible to secure a headline in the American media with a suggestion that the Russians might secure a base in Taiwan or Viet Nam. There is no prospect whatever of the former. As I mentioned earlier, the regime in Taipei has always asserted that it was the sole legitimate government of the whole of China. In the light of China's relations with Russia over not only the last half century but the last three centuries, no government claiming to govern China could accept a Russian base in its territory. Nor would this be likely to occur if Taipei renounced its claim to mainland China.

I cannot be so dogmatic in discounting the possibility of a Russian base in Viet Nam, for instance in Cam Ranh Bay or Danang. In neither place, however, would the base have a fraction of the potential of Subic Bay or Clark Field, to which the only threats can be the attitude of the local population. I regard it as singularly unlikely that Viet Nam, having fought the Americans successfully for twenty years, the French successfully for eighty years, and the Chinese successfully for many centuries in order to ensure her identity and independence, would now compromise herself by accepting foreign bases. The prospects of such a base depend upon the attitude of China and the United States. If China does not invade again, if the United States shows even a modicum of generosity to Viet Nam, I would predict there are minimal chances of the Soviet Union securing any permanent bases in Viet Nam. On the other hand, a Vietnamese conviction that China would invade again and a Chinese assertion that Viet Nam should be "taught another lesson" can only increase the possibility of a Soviet base. The fears of each side would become a self-fulfilling prophecy. The likeliest possibility is that the U.S.S.R. might arrange a facility for satellite surveillance in Viet Nam such as the United States has at San Miguel and Alice Springs.

The whole argument on bases is rather dated. Because the British set up bases around the world before World War I and the Americans did so after World War II, many people assume that the Soviet Union must be avid for bases all around the world. Modern technology, a viable tool for the Soviet Union no less than for the United States, shows that bases are less and less a military necessity. They have become politically counterproductive; in fact, the Soviet Union has had less success even than the United States has had in recent years in receiving the gratitude of those countries to which it has extended military assistance.

Now that almost every country in the world has recognized the government in Peking as the sole legitimate government of China including the province of Taiwan, it is time to remove the hindrance to regional trade and development presented by China's exclusion from the World Bank and the Asian Development Bank. China has not become one of the governments that owns the World Bank, because Taiwan, although no longer on the Board, is still a member and a borrower. In other international bodies, the whole has been substituted for the part. China might be expected to subscribe to the World Bank in lieu of Taiwan but cannot be expected to take over the loans and credits disbursed to Taiwan. China was substituted for Taiwan as a member of ESCAP in 1971; Taiwan, however, remains a member of the ADB, which was sponsored by ESCAP. Here, too, China might be expected to subscribe to the ADB in lieu of Taiwan, but she cannot be expected to be substituted as the borrower of loans extended to Taiwan in the way that Viet Nam took over the loans extended to the regime in Saigon.

Having dealt with some of the residual issues arising from the policy of dividing Korea, Viet Nam, and China for great-power purposes, I shall mention some problems that are certain to arise in the South Seas, the last colonial area in the world.

There were hostilities in the East Indies when the Netherlands, Britain, and Portugal successively extricated themselves from West New Guinea, Northern Borneo, and East Timor; in the last case, there was great loss of life, not only during the civil war but in the famine that ensued. Brunei can be expected to move tranquilly from the British to the ASEAN aegis. In the adjacent area of the South Pacific, however, the French have yet to depart.

It is difficult today to imagine the tension between Britain and France after Admiral Du Petit-Thouars made Tahiti a French protectorate in 1842 and imprisoned the British consul Pritchard in 1844. It would be impossible to rekindle the enthusiasm that

France and Britain, Germany and the United States exhibited a hundred years ago in establishing sovereignty over the Polynesian principalities and plantations. It cannot be taken for granted that France's departure will be tranquil.

Ten territories that used to be ruled by Britain, Australia, and New Zealand have now achieved independence or self-government. Western Samoa was the first to become independent in 1962 and was followed by Nauru in 1968, Fiji and Tonga in 1970, Papua New Guinea in 1975, Solomon Islands and Tuvalu (formerly the Ellice Islands) in 1978; and Kiribati (formerly the Gilbert Islands) in 1979. The Cook Islands became self-governing in 1965 and Niue in 1974. These 10 states, together with Australia and New Zealand, constitute the South Pacific Forum.

Guam and American Samoa are U.S. unincorporated territories. The United States plans to terminate her U.N. Trust Territory of the Pacific Islands (Micronesia) in 1981, when the Territory will emerge as four separate entities: the Northern Marianas, which have opted for a Commonwealth status relationship like Puerto Rico's; and Palau, the Federated States of Micronesia, and the Marshall Islands, which have chosen associated status, that is, independence in all but defense matters. Micronesia and the Marshalls have shown an interest in future participation in the South Pacific Forum.

There are three overseas territories of France: New Caledonia and Dependencies, Wallis and Futuna Islands, and French Polynesia (Tahiti). France remains tenacious of her influence and culture in the South Pacific. The historic alienation of land in New Caledonia particularly, and the more recent influx of metropolitan officials, colons from Algeria and Indo-China and Polynesians from Wallis and Futuna, have put the indigenous population in a minority and have produced a cauldron of Southern African ingredients. French naval ships are known to be in port during elections for the local assemblies and their crews are known to exercise their rights as French citizens to vote in the elections and, naturally enough, in crucial electoral districts. In recent years, France has spared no expense on education in her territories and in the New Hebrides.

The New Hebrides are a British-French condominium due to be granted independence in 1980. All current conflicts have been imported by the imperialists. They reflect the differences between British and French policies on decolonization and can be seen in the education system, the political system, the religious structure, and the public service. The French, through sins of commission, and the British, through sins of omission, have created a highly volatile situation. Following the elections for the Representative Assembly on 14 November 1979, the anglophone Vanua'aku Party formed a government with the two-thirds majority required for constitutional changes. The country is expected to become independent in May 1980 under the name Vanuatu. It will join the British Commonwealth. We may hope that the New Hebrides, having, like Mauritius and the Seychelles, both a French and a British tradition, may prove to be a bridge between the anglophone and francophone territories of the South Pacific.

Before the British and French took over from the local chiefs and kings and the Americans took over from the Spaniards, these South Pacific territories were scarcely recognizable as political entities. They are now sovereign states, many of them with membership of the United Nations. We have seen the political troubles that can arise in islands in the East Indies which were divided by Europe's empires. We cannot prudently overlook the possibility of troubles in divided archipelagos, such as the Solomons. The best way to disown the European legacy of Balkanization is to promote a regional association of these islands. The present members of the South Pacific Forum found it relatively easy to associate because they had been colonized by the members of the Commonwealth. It will require greater statesmanship for the Forum to incorporate America's territories and still greater to incorporate France's.

There are certain to be political changes in many of the countries of the Western Pacific, but few seem likely to change the general movement toward political cooperation between them. The security and prosperity of the region will depend on its political leaders' discerning the nature and consequence of the changes.

China has completed the struggle for the succession to Mao Zedong and Zhou Enlai; we shall for some time be spared the variegated vilifications of previous years. It is noteworthy that the new leaders of China have not changed the official attitude towards the Soviet Union. The governing party in Japan may lose its majority, but no foreseeable Japanese government is likely to reverse the policy of peaceful relations with its neighbors and economic cooperation with Western countries. Korea may not be united for many, many years, but it is unlikely that warfare will break out again. Nor will the members of ASEAN soon make basic changes in their political and economic orientation.

Australia, Fiji, Papua New Guinea, and Solomon Islands will become republics because of dissatisfaction with the conduct of governors-general representing the absent and impotent head of state. The New Hebrides will become independent as a republic. The great changes in Australia's perceptions of the region were made six years ago, when a new government recognized Peking, evacuated Viet Nam, liberated Papua New Guinea, negotiated the Cultural Agreement and NARA Treaty with Japan, and abandoned the White Australia immigration policy. In fact, the next government in Australia will diminish the nostalgia for trading and investment links with Britain and the United States and strengthen the trend for economic integration in the Pacific. None of the foreseeable changes of government or changes in political institutions in any of the countries of the Western Pacific are likely to make a radical change in its political attitudes towards other countries in the region. Indochina represents the only situation in which this tendency may be reversed, but this will happen only if the West and China continue their isolation and ostracism of Viet Nam. In short, there are certain to be changes in many of the countries in the region, but it is unlikely that those changes will affect the trend towards political interdependence. The changes are less likely to represent any net aversion or disadvantage to the United States than will be the case with changes in any other region of the world.

FOUR

Australia and Japan: Two Pacific Powers

After this discussion of the resources, the trade, and the political dynamics of the Western Pacific, it may be useful to examine specifically the interrelationships between two of the developed countries of that region—Australia and Japan, two countries whose political and economic interest in each other has been promoted by many U.S. corporations and by successive U.S. administrations since the 1950s. Japan is Australia's principal customer and, after the United States, Australia's principal supplier. Australians, and Americans too, must recognize that Japan will not be content to consider her trading relationships on a bilateral basis but will increasingly insist on a regional basis. We must note that Japan sees the importance of the Western Pacific as a region. Japan is deficient in natural resources. Her major resource is human: Japanese society is well-educated and cohesive, with a long history of nationhood. Australia is a relatively new nation, but one with great mineral and energy resources— iron ore, coal, natural gas, bauxite, copper, manganese. There is, thus, a natural partnership between Japan and Australia. Australia and Japan were made into partners by American investors who extracted Australian minerals and exported them to Japan. Japanese companies soon took initiatives to develop this triangular relationship.

There are similarities between Japan's and Australia's political institutions. These may lead both nations to exaggerate the things they have in common and to overlook the things on which they differ. In the 1960s, Australia tended to exaggerate her identity with Malaysia and Singapore since, as part of the common impereial heritage, all three had apparently similar legislative and financial systems. In the same way it is possible that Australian ties with Japan may obscure our perceptions of political developments in Japan. We are lulled by the thought that, while Japan changes her prime ministers as often as Australia, the system remains unchanged. One is bound to point out, however, that political differences in Japan are greater than they appear to be because the parliamentary system there, like the parliamentary systems of Queensland and Western Australia, the two Australian States whose mineral resources find their greatest market in Japan, is distorted by gross imbalance in the population of the various electoral districts. While I do not believe that a change of government is imminent in Japan, I must also note that, when it comes, the Japanese public service might find it more difficult to adjust than has been the case in Australia.

Australia now takes a much closer interest in Japan's economy than heretofore. We tenaciously clung to Britain's imperial robes for several years following World War II, even after they became threadbare and, throughout the 1960s, we clung to America's coattails, even when the stains were showing. John McEwen, Australian Minister for Trade from December 1949 to February 1971, received little support from either side of politics in Australia when he sponsored the Japan-Australia Trade Agreement in 1957. (He was as far-sighted in his attitudes towards the advantages of trade with Japan as he was short-sighted in his attitudes towards the expansion of the European Community throughout the 1960s.)

Australia may well envy Japan's economy more than that of any nation in the world. Even so, Japanese economic success as a nation is not due, as the present Australian government would have it thought, to a small and restricted public sector. Japan's public sector appears small because Japanese companies provide many of the social services that in Australia are provided by governments. According to the OECD, in the three years to 1976, total Australian public spending was 33 percent of GDP, up 6 percentage points from the level for the three years to 1969. In Japan in the same period there was the same increase of 6 percentage points, in her case to 25 percent of GDP. Lest it be thought that the total and not the increase is significant it must be pointed out that, in the same period, the OECD average was 41 percent—up 7 percentage points—and that in West Germany, the other most admired economy, public spending averaged 44 percent, up 9 percentage points.[1]

There are many sections of the Australian community that have a long way to go before there can be an adequate national understanding of Japan. Many persons in industry and the federal public service and the academic world have acquired a better understanding than have most ministers, federal and state, and trade unionists. Most ministers and our most protected industries still hanker after the investment, trading, and political arrangements that are now in inevitable decline. Trade unionists are much better acquainted with industrial arrangements in the United States or Britain or the Soviet Union than with those in Japan or West Germany. In Japan, there is a degree of cooperation between unions and private corporations based on a feeling of mutual obligation to be found in no other industrialized society; industrial disruption is rarely evident in Japan outside the public utilities.

It is often suggested by American and Australian businessmen that their Japanese counterparts have "let us down" in contractual relationships. Japanese steel firms import their iron ore not only from Australia but also from India, Peru, and Brazil, and they obviously hope to develop some added Chinese sources in the 1980s. Producers and users of iron ore and other raw materials in the Pacific area have learnt, in the 1970s, that contracts for the movement of specified quantities between the parties over long periods of time provide rather less security than was originally hoped. From time to time, one party or the other has demanded to be relieved of the obligations in such contracts. When the

material has been in strong demand in world markets, the seller
has often found reasons for asking to be relieved of its commitments to deliver, while the buyer has usually backed away in
periods of slack demand. Agreements on prices contained in such
long-term contracts have offered no more security to the parties,
as a rule, than the agreements on quantities. As world prices have
changed, one party or the other has backed away from its price
commitments, forcing a renegotiation of the contract.

I venture the view that, in the English-speaking world, we have
been much inclined to stress the letter of the law; if at a favorable
period one makes a deal, one must stick to the terms even in a
bad time. The Japanese, on the other hand, are not literalist or
pedantic: they have vague terms in contracts but aim to have
honorable understandings with the countries with which they
deal and allow for changes in the course of a continuing relationship. They expect their suppliers, too, to adjust to new situations.
In such a relationship, they must make sure that they understand
and can trust the people with whom they are negotiating. They
want prosperity for those with whom they deal as well as for
themselves. It is not correct or fair to accuse them of "letting us
down."

Japan's economic success as a nation is due to the coordination
of the resources of government and industry, of the trade union
movement, and of the academic world. In this way, the Japanese
make a joint examination of their internal problems and opportunities and an assessment of the problems and opportunities
they understand to be arising for them externally. Once the process of consultation has been followed, then the hard decisions are
taken, if necessary, through legislative means. There is, in fact, a
much greater degree of intervention by government in Japan in
terms of deciding the allocation and distribution of resources
than has even been attempted in Australia.

Australia's dealings with Japan in the exploitation of resources
are made more difficult and confusing by Australia's federal
system. No governor in the United States and no premier in
Canada would embark on the course of national disloyalty pursued

by the premiers of Queensland and Western Australia. In Japan, it is thought to be as natural for purchasers of Australian resources to coordinate their activities as in Australia it should be regarded as natural for the vendors of those resources to coordinate theirs. Before the Labor Federal Government came to office in Australia, we saw, for instance, how Nippon Steel negotiated contracts on behalf of all Japan's steel mills for the purchase of Australian coal and iron ore and picked off Australian producers one by one. The Japanese government had MITI, the Ministry of International Trade and Industry, as its sole negotiator, whereas six "Australian" governments cut each others' throats in offering the best deal to Japanese buyers. The state governments, of course, had no concern for the prices of mineral exports, as most of their royalties were a function of volume rather than profitability. The state governments levied royalties on the volume; the federal government levied taxes on the profits. Thus, the lower the prices were, the more minerals were exported and the more royalties paid. The irresponsibility of shipping out vast amounts of underpriced minerals and accelerating the depletion of reserves did not concern the states. While in New South Wales royalties represented 15 percent of mine production less salaries and wages in 1968, in Western Australia the figure was only 7 percent, and in Queensland it was a negligible and negligent 0.8 percent.[2] When we came to office in December 1972, Japanese buyers were paying Australian coal producers 22 percent less than the average price paid to other suppliers.[3]

Under the 1968–1969 federal-state agreement on offshore petroleum resources, states were required to forward all records and reports on offshore exploration by oil companies, but in 1971 and 1972 the Director of the Bureau of Mineral Resources reported to the federal government that Western Australia, South Australia, New South Wales, and Queensland were all acting in breach of the agreement and failing to provide sufficient information. Thus, the federal government had no idea whatsoever of the extent of Australia's offshore oil reserves, particularly in the Northwest Shelf. It was not until 1973 that a satisfactory flow of information to the federal government about the shelf commenced. Western Australia again breached the federal-state agreement by unilaterally granting oil exploration permits in October 1974 without federal approval, requiring from the permittees barely sufficient exploration work to keep one drilling vessel operating, in areas where gas, not oil, would be likely to be found. Eight months later, that state's government announced that it would "go it alone" on development of the Northwest Shelf. It still maintains that desire and pretense.

The treachery of the states lay not just in breaching agreements but in the unbridled opposition and unprincipled challenges to each major piece of legislation in the minerals area, except the Pipeline Authority Act, and in the obsessive courting and succoring of overseas interests: in 1973–1974 in Western Australia, 56 percent of value added in mining was under foreign ownership and 44 percent was under foreign control, while, in Queensland, 63 percent was under foreign ownership and 84 percent was under foreign control.[4] It now appears that the Premier of Queensland would prefer a company to have its head office in Tokyo or London than in another Australian state. The divisiveness of Australia's federal system has eroded the ability of the Australian government to deal seriously with international and regional trading issues.

Japan has become Australia's major trading partner, taking 34 percent of our exports and supplying 21 percent of our imports.[5] Australia is Japan's most important supplier of raw materials, and Japan is Australia's most important single customer. In such conditions, it is natural that Japan should look to Australia for contractual security of supply and that Australia should look to Japan for contractual security of market access. In such conditions, it is natural that the present Deputy Prime Minister, who is the Minister for Trade and Resources, should seek to enforce the mineral export guidelines initiated by my minister: no one could describe the interaction of Australian ore and coal producers with Japanese steel mills as a manifestation of the perfect competition model. In such conditions, it is natural that Australia should seek,

and obtain, access to Japanese markets for Australian fish harvested by Australian boats that is equal to the access afforded
Australian fish harvested by Japanese boats. And, in such conditions, it is remarkable that Australia has no long-term planning
facilities in the image of Japan's. Not only is the extent of public
planning limited to the attention span of senior government officials, but private planning in both Australia and Japan is severely
inhibited by the refusal of Australia's Treasury to publish detailed
forecasts of the Australian economy. In view of the recent long
sequence of failures of such forecasts, this objection to public
scrutiny comes as no surprise, but it is certainly time it was over-
turned.

The experience of close trade contact with Japan has not
conditioned Australians to look at the world in breadth or
depth. The importance of Japan to Australia—and of Australia to
Japan—has become such a truism that many Australians have
come to have the same myopic enthusiasm for Japan as we have
had in the past for Britain and the United States. Japan has been
seen as the be-all and end-all of our prosperity and economic
security.

Up to the mid-1970s, there were growing ties between Australia and the ASEAN countries. Both ASEAN and Australia
thought that there were mutual advantages in their discussing the
relations of each with the rest of the world. There were still some
misgivings in ASEAN about Japan's trade practices. The position
has since greatly changed. Meetings now take place between
Japanese and ASEAN Prime Ministers and other ministers more
regularly than they take place between the Japanese or ASEAN
ministers and their Australian counterparts.

Japan and Australia are only two in a region of over a dozen
nations in the Western Pacific rim. It is time for Australians to
recognize the very great opportunities awaiting them and respon-
sibilities facing them regarding trade with countries that were
once colonies of Japan—Korea, Taiwan—or enemies of Japan—
China—or within the envisaged Greater East Asia Co-Prosperity
Sphere. As it is, Australia's real trade with the developing East

Asian nations is increasing at three to four times the rate of increase in Australia's trade with Japan.

This increasing economic intradependence in the Western Pacific region derives from a number of related factors. The dissolution of the great European empires of the past removed, in spirit at least, the dependency of the structures of colonial economies upon the structures of the patron economies. It is no coincidence that regional identity is reasserting itself in East Asia at the same time that it is doing so in Africa and in Europe. Technological developments in transport and communication have made it far cheaper to send goods by ship than by any other means and much easier to communicate across the seas than in the past. The rapid economic growth experienced by the developing countries of the region in particular has generated increasing intra-regional trade and been generated by it.

Now the regional economy is entering a period of structural change. The developing East Asian countries have become extremely proficient in the production of a whole range of labor-intensive manufactures. The more rapidly growing of these countries—that is, those that embarked earliest on export-oriented manufacturing strategies—are advancing into capital-intensive manufactures as wages increase, and the later developers begin to build up their own manufacturing sectors.

The Japanese economy is divesting itself of its labor-intensive and energy-intensive industries as they become increasingly subjected to import competition from developing East Asia and important criticism from the Japanese electorate; her economy is shifting towards the production of "knowledge-intensive" goods. Whereas, until recently, Japan has been primarily an importer of raw materials from the region, she is now becoming an extensive importer of a number of labor-intensive and capital-intensive manufactures.

In the Australian economy, broadly based manufacturing industry has been developed behind high protective barriers. As the inefficiency of these industries has become more pronounced and their operations have become less profitable, employment in them has fallen. Investment funds have been channeled away from manufacturing into mining, lured by the incentives offered by various Liberal Governments. The direct and indirect employment benefits of Australia's mining industry have been far from overwhelming, even though Australia has been extracting its mineral resources at a much faster rate than the rest of the world. (Australia has only 11 percent of world bauxite reserves but is responsible for an immense 30 percent of world bauxite production. She has 24 percent of brown coal reserves but 35 percent of brown coal production; 5 percent of iron ore reserves but 11 percent of iron ore production; she has 7 percent of ilmenite ore reserves but 27 percent of ilmenite production; 3 percent of nickel reserves but 10 percent of nickel production; 2 percent of tin reserves but 6 percent of tin production; 29 percent of rutile reserves and an incredible 97 percent of rutile production.)[6] By the end of the century, Australia will have exhausted her supplies of tin and nickel and probably rutile—though the other producers of the world will have another fifty years' worth of these minerals left—because of the subsidies and laissez-faire exploitation policies of present and previous conservative governments.

Over the next ten years, particularly after a change of government, we can expect Australian manufacturing to move towards more specialized and export-oriented production. In addition, we can expect growth in Australia of resource-based, export-oriented manufactures, such as metals processing, in order to benefit from the increasing comparative advantage Australia does and will hold in this form of production.

Australia and Japan, as developed countries, have the opportunity, and, indeed, the responsibility, to build up the economic base of the region. I do not wish to disparage or downgrade Australia's relationship with Japan, but I observe that Japan to a certain extent already is taking a wider view of her own opportunities and obligations in Southeast Asia. If Australia does not adjust her economy to take account and advantage of the changes in the developed and developing parts of the regional economy, she will find herself, so to speak, left out on a rim. She cannot rely upon the export of industrial raw materials to Japan to provide a long-term stimulus to the Australian economy, as the era of rapid growth in the Japanese mineral-processing industry has ended.

Yet, the longer Australia maintains her high protective wall against Asian manufactured imports, the more incensed will Australian consumers become at the inflated prices they pay for clothing and other goods and the more alienated and infuriated will developing Asian neighbors become at this isolationist and indeed futile stance. Those neighbors reacted in a vehement and united fashion against Australia's proposals to lower air fares on through flights by the Australian airline and the European airlines between Australia and Europe. They were alienated and infuriated by the assumption that their own airlines could be excluded, their transit facilities taken for granted, and their tourist attractions ignored.

Japan's highly protectionist agricultural policies are little or no better. It is remarkable that Japanese consumers pay up to five times the amounts that Australian consumers pay for their meat. It might be possible to feel sympathy for such policies if Japan were suffering severe balance-of-payment difficulties. Japanese officials overseas must find it embarrassingly difficult to justify such policies in the light of her enormous trading surpluses. The recent depreciation of the Japanese currency and the commencement of monthly balance-of-payments deficits have helped to ameliorate this embarrassment, though not the problem of agricultural protectionism.

The worst excesses in Australian protection policy have resulted from attempts to reduce the rapid fall in employment in certain industries, and in general these excesses are consequences of Australia's high rate of unemployment. This protection has increased inflation and hence costs to producers in Australia. It has also aggravated the deficit which developing Asian economies have in their trade with Australia at a time when the balance of trade is 3 to 2 in Australia's favor. Asia's natural response to this situation is obviously not to open the door to further Australian imports but, instead, to erect barriers to their entry. This reaction will be exacerbated by the fall in demand for Asian exports generated by the depression in the Australian economy itself. In a highly interdependent regional economy, unemployment in a major economy such as Australia's can thereby result in her export sector failing to operate at full potential or even declining.

The point I am making is that the popular rationale supporting the "reduce inflation first at the expense of employment" strategy—namely, that it is the only means to increase the overseas competitiveness of Australia's industries—is fallacious. If exchange-rate controls are employed judiciously, inflation may well have a less deleterious effect on the trading situation than widespread unemployment would. We can well refer back to the worldwide protectionist reactions to the unemployment levels of the 1930s, perhaps the most crippling barriers erected against trade in twentieth-century history. Western governments in general should consider the possibility of increasing low-cost imports as a tool for reducing contemporary cost-push inflation. This would promote economic growth in the developing countries, providing markets for exporters in the developed countries and thus allowing economic growth in the West to continue. The alternative generally practiced—even harsher fiscal and monetary policies—harms everyone and is of little utility in reducing inflation.

We should have no illusions that the propping up of beleaguered industries can ameliorate unemployment. In Australia between 1972-1973 and 1975-1976, the industries that suffered the greatest decline in employment were those that had the greatest protection or subsidization by the Australian community. Yet this decline was not because they suffered from import competition; in fact, these industries were subjected to the smallest increase in competition from imports owing to special efforts to protect them after the onset of recession.[7]

Protection failed to protect jobs for two reasons. First, the most heavily protected industries are precisely those most incapable of adaptation to change. Second, they are industries whose aim is generally to serve only the domestic market. Once growth reaches its market limits, investment expenditure in these industries becomes a means not of developing new products or processes or increasing production runs but simply of replacing workers by machinery. Thus, we can witness that the most rapid rate of labor replacement occurs in the most protected industries[8] —industries that in many cases enjoy higher rates of profitability than manufacturing as a whole[9] (and industries that are, incidentally, less, not more, decentralized than less protected manufacturing industries).[10] High tariffs do nothing to preserve jobs. On the contrary, they represent a threat to jobs: they not only transfer income from poor consumers to rich consumers (through the higher tariffs on goods that are, like clothing, relatively income-inelastic) but also, through accelerating the replacement of labor, transfer income from workers to shareholders.

Many people take the view that increasing protection is necessary to prevent the Australian economy from being dominated by transnationals. They argue that, because transnationals are taking up an increasing proportion of world trade, then decreasing Australia's involvement in the world economy is necessary to preserve national economic sovereignty. Such arguments essentially ignore the ability of transnationals to dominate industries oriented towards domestic production as easily as they dominate industries oriented towards trade and to do so with substantial protection paid for by consumers. There is virtually no correlation between levels of local or foreign ownership and levels of protection afforded an industry in Australia.[11]

The only way transnationals can be constrained is by direct government regulation. Arbitrary imposition or tariffs merely leads to these companies redirecting their production strategies, not to the benefit of the local population but to the sole benefit of themselves.

I have already mentioned how Japan and Australia, as advanced industrialized nations, have the opportunity to develop the economy of the region. In addition, however, again in their roles as advanced industrialized countries, they have the responsibility to ensure a more equitable distribution of the region's affluence.

While there is a harmony of interest in increased economic growth in the region, there is also a conflict of interest between the developed and developing nations of the region, a microcosm of the global North-South dispute. While I do not wish to elaborate here on the details of the North-South conflict, the importance of a new international economic order to developing nations in our region, particularly the ASEAN nations, would be hard to over-estimate. UNCTAD figures show that, if we add up the value of world trade in the 18 commodities that will be included in the Common Fund, Malaysia is the second most affected country in the world (behind Brazil), with the Philippines third, Indonesia seventh, and Thailand thirteenth.[12]

It is also important to note that Japan has been a vital importer of developing nations' raw materials, and fluctuations in her demand for them can have pervasive effects upon the exporting nations' economies. A turnaround in Japanese demand meant that the price received for timber in Malaysia, Indonesia, and the Philippines fell during 1974 to a little over one-third its previous level, while, during the same period, the world price for copper exported by the Philippines, Indonesia, and Papua New Guinea also fell to barely one-third its previous level. In Papua New Guinea, this resulted in a fall of total government revenues by over one-third.[13] During the copper crisis, the world price of refined copper was depressed by Japanese producers committed to importing copper ore, who turned to selling on the world market in response to falling domestic demand. It was similar in effect to the Lomé Convention's role in depressing world sugar prices. Such situations could have been ameliorated by adequate buffer stock and compensating financing arrangements for regional or world trade in such commodities. In their report to the Australian and Japanese governments in 1976, Sir John Crawford and Dr. Saburo Okita have already recommended such arrangements for bilateral trade between Australia and Japan; we should apply them throughout the region, until adequate global arrangements are made.

While these are important international issues of great significance to regional stability, the conduct of Australia and Japan in international forums has fallen far short of serving the best interests of the region. The developing countries of East Asia could be excused for thinking that the Multilateral Trade Negotiations have been a mutual arrangement among Japan, Europe, and North America to restrain them from international trade. The countries that lie between Japan and Australia are much more critical of the motives of each of us than they were in 1973 when we reduced our tariffs across the board by 20 and 25 percent respectively.

Alienation between the developed and developing nations of our region has been compounded by a few other factors. While Japan has long since displaced the United States as the major source of overseas investment funds, this investment has not been accompanied by a sensitivity for local conditions and wishes, particularly in matters of environment, local culture, working conditions and, in some countries, national sovereignty. In addition, Japan has sadly failed to meet the internationally agreed upon target for official development assistance, which is 0.7 percent of the donor nations' GDP. Japan's assistance is around one-third this target. East Asia expects and welcomes economic help from Japan more than from the United States or Western Europe. Australia, too, has disappointed Asia in this matter. Although official development assistance had climbed to 0.6 percent of Australia's GDP during my government's term of office, this figure has since fallen to 0.45 percent of GDP.[14]

So far, in discussing the past and future of Japan and Australia I have dwelt mainly on economic relations. I have long known that the relations between Australia and Japan must be more widely based—ever since I realized that, whatever may have been the failures of politicians and the intrusions of the military in pre-war Japan, the Anglo-American world, including Australia, was largely responsible for goading Japan into war by restricting her access to markets and resources. I had resolved that, when I became Prime Minister, I would take up the suggestion that Japan had made to our predecessors—and that they had rejected—to conclude a treaty of friendship, commerce, and navigation, and also to extend the relationship with Japan beyond the purely economic level. The NARA Treaty—the Nippon-Australia Relations Agreement—was a vital step for our two nations, significant also in its title because the city of Nara was the first permanent capital ever established by a government of Japan and a city which is the prime archaelogical as well as one of the prime historical sites in the country.

The Cultural Agreement, signed in 1974, was an attempt to diminish the mutual incomprehension and mutual ignorance that, for all the closeness of our economic relations, characterized our understanding of each other's societies. For the same reasons, my government initiated the Australia-Japan Foundation, aimed at promoting and fostering a continuing program to build and widen mutual contacts at all levels—business, academic, cultural, scientific, trade union. It is barbaric to assume that relations between two such countries as ours should be based purely and solely on money. I had thus attempted to begin to break down the great barriers of language, tradition, culture, and distance that separate our peoples.

(To complete the record, under my government, Australia and Japan also signed an Agreement for the Protection of Migratory Birds and Birds in Danger of Extinction and their Environment in February 1974. In April 1974, Japan informed Australia that she had completed all requirements for ratification; four years later, Australia has still not done so. It may say something of our respective perceptions that the Japanese care more about birds and Australians more about whales.)

Just as I have been anxious to stress that Japan and Australia, in discussing their economic relations, must increasingly take into account the relations each of them has with the countries that lie between them, so too each nation must develop a greater interest and sensitivity in all matters outside purely economic relations that concern those countries that lie between them. Just as the West learnt little and lost much through isolating and ostracizing Japan in the 1930s, so too has the West, including Australia, learnt little and lost much through isolating and ostracizing

China from 1949 to 1972 and Viet Nam from 1975 onwards.

The confrontation in the Korean peninsula and in Indochina, the repatriation of ethnic minorities established in the old French, British, and Dutch empires, the border disputes in Indochina and the Indonesian archipelago and the sea-bed borders through the Pacific under the emerging Law of the Sea are not problems that will diminish or disappear with the passage of time. The contending parties expect and welcome political initiatives from Japan. Japan can now exert more political influence in Southeast Asia, if she chooses to exercise it, than can China, the United States, or the U.S.S.R.; she would not arouse the same fears or resentments that each of the others would. Japan and Australia cannot afford to be inert on any of these problems. Those who are interested in Australia-Japan relations must face up to the consequences any or all of these problems can have on the relations either or both of the countries must have with all the countries that lie between them.

The relationship between Australia and Japan is in a state of transformation: the interests of both nations are diversifying in the direction of the other nations of the region. To diversify them does not mean to diminish them. On the contrary, the increasing intradependence of the Western-Pacific region means that the mutuality of Japan's and Australia's interests will not wilt but grow.

Epilogue

In announcing on 4 July 1975 Australia's contribution to the United States' upcoming Bicentennial celebrations—the endowment of a chair of Australia Studies at Harvard University—I concluded with these words: "The birth of the American Republic was one of those watersheds in human history that will be commemorated by democrats everywhere for as long as democracy survives. In two centuries, nothing has diminished the power and splendor of the words of the American Declaration of Independence, with its noble confirmation of human dignity, its unforgettable affirmation of the equality of all men and their rights to life, liberty, and the pursuit of happiness. Those words, so familiar, yet fresh and imperishable, still fire the hearts and minds of men."

Those words can continue to fire the hearts of men, not least of all in that region where the most rapid economic growth in the world is now taking place. Within that region, many states are aspiring to consummate their unity and independence. As these take their places with the long-established nations in the area, it is hoped that a Pacific Community will grow stronger, flourish, and direct its energy towards economic health and cultural understanding in a peaceful world.

Notes

Bibliography

Index

Notes

1. RESOURCES OF THE PACIFIC

1. Mahbub ul Haq, *The Poverty Curtain* (New York, 1976).
2. T.M. Fitzgerald, *The Contribution of the Mineral Industry to Australian Welfare* (Report to the Minister for Minerals and Energy, Canberra, 1974).
3. John Short, "RFX still stalks the corridors," *Australian Financial Review,* 18 January 1980.
4. The abrasive relationships between American whalers and sealers, such as Amasa and Samuel Delano, and the authorities and colonists in New South Wales are described in *Early American-Australian Relations: from the arrival of the Spaniards in America to the close of 1830* by Gordon Greenwood (Melbourne, 1944), pp. 73–90 and passim.

2. WESTERN PACIFIC TRADE

1. Ross Garnaut, "Trade Pressures from Abroad," *Economic Papers* 59, (August 1978), pp. 18–34.
2. Bank of Japan, Economic Research Department, "Hopeful Trends in Foreign Capital Inflows," in *Asia Corporate Profile and National Finance* (Manila, 1977).
3. Organization for Economic Cooperation and Development, *Main Economic Indicators* (Paris, various issues); World Bank, *Annual Report,* 1978.
4. United Nations, *Statistical Yearbook* (New York, 1967).
5. Dan Morgan, *Merchants of Grain* (New York, 1979).
6. *Far Eastern Economic Review, Asia Yearbook* (Hong Kong, 1977).
7. Mahbub ul Haq, "Negotiating a New Bargain with the Rich Countries,"

in G.F. Erb & V. Kallab, eds., *Beyond Dependency* (Washington, 1976).

8. Garnaut, "Trade Pressures."

9. Bank of Japan, "Hopeful Trends"; Asian Development Bank, *Key Indicators of Developing Member Countries,* April 1978 and October 1979.

10. Australia, *Australia Official Development Assistance to Developing Countries 1978–79* (Canberra, 1978).

11. ADB, *Key Indicators.*

12. Ho Kwon Ping, "Caught in the Oil Debt Trap," *Far Eastern Economic Review,* 19 October 1979.

13. Australia, Committee on Australia's Relations with the Third World, *Australia and the Third World* (Canberra, 1979).

14. ADB, *Key Indicators.*

15. World Bank, *Annual Report,* 1978.

16. *Asian Wall Street Journal,* 10 April 1979; OECD, *Main Economic Indicators.*

17. "The Emergence of South East Asia," *Conjoncture,* monthly economic bulletin of Banque de Paris et des Pays-Bas, No. 71, November 1978.

18. ADB, *Key Indicators.*

19. Sir John Crawford and Dr. Saburo Okita, *Australia, Japan and Western Pacific Economic Relations,* Report to the Governments of Australia and Japan (Australian Government Publishing Service, Canberra, 1976); Peter A. Drysdale and Alan G. Rix, "Australia's Economic Relations with Asia and the Pacific," *Current Affairs Bulletin* 55.11:1–15 (1 April 1979); ADB, *Key Indicators.*

20. Drysdale and Rix, "Australia's Economic Relations."

21. Australia, Bureau of Industry Economics, *Industrialisation in Asia— Some Implications for Australian Industry* (Research Report 1, Canberra, 1978).

22. Lawrence B. Krause, "The Pacific Economy in an Interdependent World," in *Vital Speeches of the Day* 45.6:170–175 (1 January 1979).

23. Fox Butterfield, "Ma was Right, the Chinese are still Breeding too Fast," *Australian Financial Review,* 14 November 1979.

24. International Confederation of Free Trade Unions, *Trade Unions and the Transnationals* (published for the Twelfth World Congress of ICFTU, Madrid, 1979).

25. Arghiri Emmanuel, *Unequal Exchange* (New York, 1972).

26. Hugh Patrick and P.A. Drysdale, "An Asia-Pacific Regional Economic Organization: An Exploratory Concept Paper" (Congressional Research Service, Library of Congress, Washington, 1979). Also published as Research Paper No. 61 by Australia-Japan Economic Relations Research Project, 1979.

27. Andrew McGregor, "The Lomé Convention and the ACP Sugar Exporters: The Political Economy of Conflicting Policies" (paper presented to the 7th Conference of Economists, Sydney, 1978).

28. United Nations Conference on Trade and Development, *UNCTAD TD/ B/C.1/166/Supp.5.*

29. G. Sacerdoti and M. Richardson, "Moving Forward Little by Little," *Far Eastern Economic Review,* 29 December 1978.

30. ADB, *Key Indicators.*

3. POLITICS OF THE WESTERN PACIFIC

1. The files dealing with these matters are not yet open to the public. On 19 August 1975, I tabled in the Parliament a paper called "Australia's Military Commitment to Viet Nam," prepared by Emeritus Professor R.G. Neale, who had been Editor of Historical Documents in the Australian Department of Foreign Affairs from 1970 and has been Director-General of the Australian Archives since 1975.

4. AUSTRALIA AND JAPAN: TWO PACIFIC POWERS

1. Organization for Economic Co-operation and Development, *Public Expenditure Trends* (Paris, 1978).

2. Alan Henderson, "Aspects of Budget Policy and the Australian Mining Industry" (MEc thesis, Monash University, Melbourne, 1971), cited in Susan Bambrick, "Mining: The Problem for Australian Governments," *Australian Quarterly* 45.1:64–77 (March 1973), p. 69.

3. "Coal: Concern over Prices," *Financial Times,* 4 September 1979.

4. Australian Bureau of Statistics, "Foreign Ownership and Control of the Mining Industry 1973–74 and 1974–75" (Canberra, 1976).

5. Drysdale and Rix, "Australia's Economic Relations."

6. Australia, Bureau of Mineral Resources, Mineral Economics Section, "Australian Identified Mineral Resources, 1978," *Australian Mineral Industry Quarterly* 31.4:177–181 (December 1978).

7. Australia, Industries Assistance Commission, *Annual Report 1977–78* (Canberra, 1978).

8. Ibid.

9. Australian Confederation of Apparel Manufacturers, "Australian Apparel Industry Facts" (Canberra, 1979); Ross Gittins, "Protection money may not really save jobs," *Sydney Morning Herald,* 13 August 1979.

10. Industries Assistance Commission, *Annual Report 1977–78.*

11. For the 12 Australian Standard Industry Classification industry groups in 1975–1976, the correlation coefficient r^2 between foreign ownership

and level of protection was only 0.02. Australian Bureau of Statistics, "Foreign Control in Manufacturing Industry: Study of Large Enterprise Groups 1975–76" (Canberra, 1978); Industries Assistance Commission, *Annual Report 1977–78.*

12. Amado Castro, "Economic Co-operation in ASEAN," (paper at 10th Pacific Trade and Development Conference, Canberra, 1979).

13. Jenny Corbett and Ross Garnaut, "Japan and the Resource-Rich Developing Countries" (Australia-Japan Economic Relations Research Project research paper, Canberra, 1976).

14. Australia, *Official Development Assistance.*

An Annotated Bibliography

Although the lectures on which this book is based were derived largely from personal observations and contacts in Australia, the United States, Japan, the ASEAN countries, and Viet Nam in 1978 and 1979, the materials listed below have also made a valuable contribution.

Since April and May 1979, when the lectures were originally delivered, the most significant new publication has been *North-South: A Programme for Survival* (London, January 1980) by the Independent Commission on International Development Issues (the Brandt Commission). The commission's 18 members included not only Willy Brandt but also former Conservative British Prime Minister Edward Heath, Indonesian Vice-President Adam Malik, and *Washington Post* publisher Katharine Graham. Its report notes a strong mutual interest between North and South in the alleviation of world poverty, stating that, if the world cannot achieve a more equitable distribution and efficient conservation of resources, it will "move towards its own destruction." The report argues against protectionism, pointing out that exports to the South during the 1973 recession saved over 3 million jobs in the North, while the loss of jobs in the North due to imports from the South was comparatively small. The report suggests reform of the international monetary system, including the formation of a World Development Fund, and the automatic transfer of funds to developing nations through a form of world taxation. It also advocates stabilization of commodities and the establishment of a regime under which transnational corporations can contribute more to development. It calls for global disarmament, noting that 5 percent of world military expenditure would be enough to meet the cost of equipping low-income countries to approach food self-sufficiency by 1990. The report also emphasizes the need for peaceful solutions to the world's energy problems.

In Australia, the most significant new document has been *Australia and the Third World* (Canberra, 1979) by the Committee on Australian Relations with the Third World (the Harries Report). This focuses on the relationship in terms of Australia's self-perceived role as a developed nation. That approach has the disadvantage of overlooking Australia's susceptibility to some of the problems that face Third World countries and Australia's geographic position in a region of developing nations. Nonetheless, the report makes a number of important recommendations on protection, aid, Australia's stance in international negotiations, and other matters.

OFFICIAL DOCUMENTS

Asian Development Bank. *Annual Report.* Manila, various issues.

——. *Key Indicators of Developing Member Countries of ADB.* Manila, semi-annual.

——. *Basic Documents of the Asian Development Bank.* Manila, 1976. [Contains the agreement establishing the ADB, the by-laws of the ADB, the rules of the Boards of Governors and Directors, and the agreement with the Philippines regarding the ADB headquarters.]

——. "Fisheries Development Project in the Socialist Republic of Viet Nam for OPEC Special Fund Financing." Manila, February 1978.

Australia. *Australian Official Development Assistance to Developing Countries.* Canberra (formerly *Australia's External Aid*), annual. [Budget Paper detailing Australia's aid program.]

Australia, Ad-Hoc Working Committee on Australia-Japan Relations. *Australia-Japan Relations.* Canberra, 1977 (the Myer Report). [Makes recommendations for greater economic ties and social links between Australia and Japan and for machinery to improve the efficiency of governmental management.]

Australia, Bureau of Industry Economics. *Industrialisation in Asia—Some Implications for Australian Industry.* Research Report 1, Canberra, 1978. [Looks at changes in the East Asian economy and their impact upon Australia, advocating structural changes in the Australian economy to take advantage of this growth.]

Australia, Bureau of Mineral Resources, Mineral Economics Section. "Australian Identified Mineral Resources, 1978," *Australian Mineral Industry Quarterly* 31.4 (December 1978).

Australia, Committee on Australia's Relations with the Third World. *Australia and the Third World.* Canberra, 1979.

Australia, Department of Foreign Affairs. *Third United Nations Conference on the Law of the Sea.* Reports of the Australian delegation to each session. Canberra.

——. "Australia's Military Commitment to Viet Nam." Canberra, tabled in the House of Representatives, 19 August 1975. [Chronicles the deceit surrounding the announcements regarding Australia's involvement in Viet Nam, based upon official documents.]

Australia, Industries Assistance Commission. *Annual Report.* Canberra, various issues. [Presents a wide range of statistics on tariff and other forms of protection in Australian manufacturing industry in support of reductions in protection.]

Australia, Joint Committee on Foreign Affairs and Defence. *Australia, Antarctica and the Law of the Sea.* Interim Report. Canberra, 1978. [Discusses the establishment of a 200-mile EEZ around Australia's coastline and the future of Antarctica.]

Australia, Senate Standing Committee on Foreign Affairs and Defence. *Australia and the South Pacific.* Canberra, 1978.

Australian Bureau of Statistics. "Foreign Ownership and Control of the Mining Industry 1973-74 and 1974-75." Canberra, 1976. [Provides statistics on foreign ownership and control in mining by industry, country of ownership or control, degree of influence of investors, and state. Data on foreign ownership in secondary industry are provided in their "Foreign Control in Manufacturing Industry: Study of Large Enterprise Groups 1975-76." Canberra, 1978.]

Crawford, Sir John, and Dr. Saburo Okita. *Australia, Japan and Western Pacific Relations.* Report to the Governments of Australia and Japan. Australian Government Publishing Service, Canberra, 1976. [Reports on interdependence between Australia and Japan, the implications for other countries, and suggested policy responses. Contains 11 commissioned papers and an annotated list of productions of the Australia-Japan Economic Relations Research Project published in Canberra and Tokyo up until January 1976. In 1979 Dr. Okita became Japan's Foreign Minister.]

Drysdale, Peter, and Hugh Patrick. "An Asian-Pacific Regional Economic Organization: An Exploratory Concept Paper." Congressional Research Service, Library of Congress, Washington D.C., 1979. [Also published as Research Paper No. 61 by Australia-Japan Economic Relations Research Project, Canberra, 1979. Urges American support for an OPTAD but by use of arguments which will not and should not meet with favor in developing Asia: "OPTAD could be a useful vehicle for the effective revitalization of United States economic leadership in the Asian-Pacific region. In asserting its commitment to the trade and development objectives of Asian-Pacific countries, the United States could insert its own conception of Pacific needs and interests alongside those of the Western Pacific countries."]

Fitzgerald, T.M. *The Contribution of the Mineral Industry to Australian*

Welfare. Report to the Minister for Minerals and Energy. Canberra, 1974. [Describes in detail the extent to which Australian taxpayers were subsidizing the profits accruing to overseas-owned mining corporations, and recommends changes that were largely adopted by the Australian Labor Government.]

International Monetary Fund. "Socialist Republic of Viet Nam: Recent Economic Developments." Report SM/77/249. Washington, October 1977.

McNamara, Robert S. "Address to the Board of Governors." World Bank, Belgrade, 1979.

Organization for Economic Co-operation and Development. *Main Economic Indicators*. Paris, various issues. [Monthly statistics on OECD economies.]

——. *Public Expenditure Trends*. Paris, 1978. [Describes the growth in public expenditure in Western industrial nations.]

——. Chairman of the Development Assistance Committee, "OPEC Aid to the Developing Countries," *OECD Observer* 95 (November 1978). [Briefly examines the type and level of development assistance provided by each OPEC member to developing countries, and mentions in passing cooperation between OPEC and the DAC.]

South Pacific Forum. "South Pacific Forum Fisheries Agency: Draft Convention." Honiara, 1979.

United Nations. *Transnational Corporations in World Development, A Reexamination*. Commission of Transnational Corporations, New York, 1978. [Identifies problems associated with transnational corporations in the areas of transfer pricing, patents, technology transfer, agglomeration, controls on imports, exports and production, and the bargaining power of host countries. Says that, although most developing countries had attained political independence by the late 1960s, "a sense of powerlessness in the economic sphere remains predominant."]

World Bank. *Annual Report*. Washington D.C., various issues.

World Bank. "The Socialist Republic of Viet Nam: An Introductory Economic Report." Report 1718–VN. Washington, August 1977.

OTHER PUBLICATIONS

Allen, K. Radway. "Australian Fisheries in a Changing World," *Current Affairs Bulletin* 56.10 (1 March 1980). [Discusses the problems Australia will face in implementing its EEZ and the effects of the EEZ upon the fishing industry. Its reference to assurances on Australian access to Japanese fish markets, however, should be read in conjunction with Susan Woods, "Australia loses out on Japanese Market in New Fishing Treaty," *Australian Financial Review*, 18 October 1979.

Australian Broadcasting Commission. *Political Economy of Development.* Sydney, 1977. [Transcripts of eight ABC radio programs on Third World issues, including discussions with Mahbub ul Haq, Debesh Bhattacharya, Barrie Dyster, Cheryl Payer, André Gunder Frank, Ted Wheelwright, Jan Tinbergen, E.F. Schumacher, Bruce McFarlane, and Geoffrey Barraclough. In 1980, the ABC produced six tapes entitled "Australia's Asian Future" on the implications of economic developments in Asia for Australia and for Asia itself.]

Australian Confederation of Apparel Manufacturers. "Australian Apparel Industry Facts." Canberra, 1979. [Propaganda pamphlet produced by clothing, textile, and footwear industries.]

Bambrick, Susan. "Mining: the Problems for Australian Governments," *Australian Quarterly* 45.1 (March 1973). [Describes some of the problems facing the then-incoming Labor Government with regard to the mineral industry.]

Bank of Japan, Economic Research Department. "Hopeful Trends in Foreign Capital Inflows," *Asia Corporate Profile and National Finance.* Manila, 1977. [Foreign investment in East Asia.]

Barnet, Richard J. and Ronald E. Müller. *Global Reach: The Power of the Multinational Corporation.* New York, Simon & Schuster, 1974.

Bergin, Anthony. "Frozen Assets—Resource Problems and Australia," *Dyason House Papers* 6.1 (September 1979). [Suggests a condominium arrangement for governing Antarctica involving the Treaty Parties only, but with provision for global supervision of its activities and international distribution of Antarctica's fruits.]

Bhattacharya, Debesh. "Aggression by the Rich Countries against the Poor: What Has UNCTAD IV Achieved?" World Christian Action, Australian Catholic Relief and Action for World Development, Sydney, 1976. [Puts the South's case for a new international economic order and describes the South's frustration at UNCTAD IV in Nairobi, 1976.]

Boyce, P.J. "Great Powers in the South Pacific," *World Review* 18.3 (August 1979). [Describes the interest shown of late in the island states of the Pacific by Australia, New Zealand, U.S.A., U.S.S.R., France, Great Britain, Japan, China, and West Germany.]

Butterfield, Fox. "Ma was Right, the Chinese are still Breeding too Fast," *Australian Financial Review,* 14 November 1979.

Cameron, C.R. "Grappling with the Giants," *Australian Business Law Review* 1.4 (December 1973). [The then Minister for Labour urges the development of international links between trade unions and the appointment of workers to boards of large enterprises.]

Carey, Alex and Marion Hosking. "Rewriting the Vietnam War," *New Journalist* 32 (May 1979). [Explains how attempts in the popular media in Australia and the United States to portray participation in the Viet Nam

War in a favorable light have colored reporting on other issues such as the Kampuchea conflict and the refugee problem.]

Castro, Amado. "Economic Co-operation in ASEAN." Paper at 10th Pacific Trade and Development Conference, Canberra, 1979. [A brief resumé of economic cooperation in ASEAN by a member of the ASEAN secretariat.]

"Coal: Concern over Prices," *Financial Times,* 4 September 1979. [Part of the informative *Financial Times* supplement on Australia.]

"Collapse of the Grain Talks: the Reasons Why," *International Development Review* 21.2 (1979). [Briefly discusses the reasons for the breakdown of negotiations on treaties for wheat, coarse grains, and food aid, emphasizing the problems caused by the United States, Canada, Australia, Argentina, the EEC, and Japan excluding developing countries from the core of the negotiations.]

Corbett, Jenny and Ross Garnaut. "Japan and the Resource-Rich Developing Countries." Australia-Japan Economic Relations Research Project Research Paper, Canberra, 1976. [Examines the implications of Japan's emergence as a major raw material importer, including the problems Japan's growth has created for domestic inequality, economic instability, and political sovereignty in developing countries while arguing that none of these inevitably follow increases in resource trade, foreign investment, or aid.]

Crittenden, Ann. "Dismal Track Record of Trade Sanctions" *Australian Financial Review,* 14 January 1980; also *New York Times,* 13 January 1980. [Discusses the failure of trade sanctions through recent history. Written in the context of the Iran-U.S. crisis, but equally relevant for Viet Nam-U.S. relations.]

Cuddy, J.D.A. "The Case for an Integrated Programme for Commodities," *Resources Policy* 5.1 (March 1979). [An UNCTAD official argues that the proposed IPC would "bring net benefits to all participants" and that many of the objections to the IPC/Common Fund proposals are fallacious.]

Dahlby, Tracy. "A Headlong Drive for Exports in a Race Against the Clock," *Far Eastern Economic Review,* 15 February 1980. [Provides, as of time of going to press, the most recent description of developments in the world automobile industry, in particular of Japanese firms' attempts to set up overseas production.]

Davies, Derek. "Exploiting the Pacific Tide," *Far Eastern Economic Review,* 21 December 1979. [Describes progress towards a Pacific Community concept as of that date. *FEER* is most useful for keeping up to date on this subject.]

Delamaide, Darrell. "The Sad Side of Mergers," *Australian Financial Review,*

8 November 1979. [Recent evidence in support of government regulation of large national and transnational corporations. Report of a survey that shows that mergers and takeovers do not result in improved efficiency, lower prices, expanded sales, higher profits, or increased benefits for the consumer.]

Dixon, G.L.R., and V.J. McGown. "The Behaviour of Australian Manufactured Exports 1968-69–1972-73." Paper presented to 49th ANZAAS Congress, Auckland, 1979. [Emphasizes the high rate of growth in Australian non-resource-based manufactured exports, often overlooked. Argues that Australia can benefit by concentrating upon industries that are intensive in "human capital" (trained or educated labor) as a basis for export growth. Indicates, by implication, both the necessity for tariff reductions and the necessity for appropriate retraining of the affected work force.]

Drysdale, Peter A. "An Organisation for Pacific Trade, Aid and Development: Regional Arrangements and the Resource Trade." Australia-Japan Economic Relations Research Project, Research Paper No. 49. Canberra, 1978. [Reviews from an Australian perspective the history of the OPTAD concept, and describes some positive roles such an organization might play, particularly with regard to resources trade.]

Drysdale, Peter A, and Kiyoshi Kojima, eds. *Australia-Japan Economic Relations in the International Context: Recent Experience and the Prospects Ahead.* Australia-Japan Economic Relations Research Project, Canberra and Tokyo, 1978. [Contains readings on Australia-Japan economic relations, the Japanese economy, the Australian minerals industry, trade in coal, implications of industrialization for the Australian economy, and trade between the EEC and Japan.]

Drysdale, Peter A., and Alan G. Rix. "Australia's Economic Relations with Asia and the Pacific," *Current Affairs Bulletin* 55.11 (1 April 1979). [Analyzes past and future trends in Pacific economic relations and Australia's role in them, emphasizing the growing interdependence and development of the regional economy, and suggesting the establishment of a "regional organization aimed at providing a firm framework for growing regional interdependence."]

Edwards, Clive T. "The Impact of Economic Change in Asia on Australia." Paper presented to Conference of Labor Economists, Adelaide, 1979. [Advocates changes in government intervention to make Australian industry more trade-oriented. Similar articles can be found in *Australian Economic Review,* 1st quarter 1978, and *Australian Bulletin of Labour* 4.3 (June 1978).

"The Emergence of Southeast Asia," *Conjuncture,* monthly economic bulletin of the Banque de Paris et des Pays-Bas, 71 (November 1978).

[Summarizes recent growth in GDP, exports, and imports in Japan and developing East Asia.]

Emmanuel, Arghiri. *Unequal Exchange.* New York, Monthly Review Press, 1972. [A theoretical treatise that describes how differing wage levels in developed and developing countries lead to unequal exchange in trade.]

English, H. Edward. "ASEAN's Quest for Allocative Efficiency in Manufacturing." Paper presented at 10th Pacific Trade and Development Conference, Canberra, 1979. [Examines the structure of comparative advantage within ASEAN countries, and suggests as an afterthought that Japan and the United States should make parallel bilateral offers to reduce non-tariff barriers to trade as an example for other regions or countries of a means of heading towards a resolution of the North-South conflict.]

Ford, Glyn and Michael Gibbons. "Whose Nodules are They?," *New Scientist* 82.1156 (24 May 1979). [Briefly describes the consortiums planning deep sea bed mining and the technical difficulties to be overcome.]

Freudenberg, Graham. "The Australian Labor Party and Vietnam," *Australian Outlook* 33.2 (August 1979). [Discusses the ALP's opposition to and the Liberal Government's support for involvement in Viet Nam and the tendency both parties had to focus their attitudes "almost exclusively through the lens of the American alliance." Concludes that, "to the extent that the Australian Labor Party did warn that America could be weakened and could be humiliated in Viet Nam, that party can claim to have been a better friend to America and the alliance."]

Garnaut, Ross. "Trade Pressures from Abroad," *Economic Papers* 59 (August 1978). [Discusses changes in Australia's international economic environment, and possible policy responses.]

Garnaut, Ross, and Kym Anderson. "ASEAN Export Specialization and the Evolution of Comparative Advantage in the Western Pacific Region." Paper presented to 10th Pacific Trade and Development Conference, Canberra, 1979. [A neo-classical analysis of changes in comparative advantage in the Western Pacific region.]

Gittins, Ross. "Protection money may not really save jobs," *Sydney Morning Herald,* 13 August 1979.

Greenwood, Gordon. *Early American-Australian Relations: from the arrival of the Spaniards in America to the close of 1830.* Melbourne, The University of Melbourne Press, 1944.

Gregory, R.G., and L.D. Martin. "An Analysis of Relationships between Import Flows to Australia and Recent Exchange Rate and Tariff Charges," *Economic Record* 52.1 (March 1976). [Shows that tariff charges had a much smaller effect upon import flows than changes in currency valuation and domestic demand in the period 1969–1974, refuting many of the claims that have been made about the effect of the 1973 25% tariff cuts upon unemployment.]

Greig, D.W. "Territorial Sovereignty and the Status of Antarctica," *Australian Outlook* 32.2 (August 1978). [Examines the legal basis of claims to territory in the Antarctic. Although generally glossing over the consequences of Third World pressure on the subject of Antarctica, concludes that territorial claims in Antarctica are "less than sovereign."]

Gruen, F.H. "The 25% Tariff Cut; Was it a Mistake?" *Australian Quarterly* 47.2 (June 1975). [Discusses the impact of the 1973 tariff cut and concludes that it was not a mistake.]

Guest, Iain. "North Versus South," *Round Table,* 273 (January 1979). [Chronicles the "sad demise of the new international economic order" with special mention of the role of the United States.]

Gulland, John. "The New Ocean Regime: Winners and Losers," *Ceres* 12.4 (July/August 1979). [A very brief summary of implications of the new ocean fisheries regime.]

Haq, Mahbub Ul. "Negotiating a New Bargain with the Rich Countries," G.F. Erb and V. Kallab, eds., *Beyond Dependency.* Overseas Development Council, Washington, 1976.

——. *The Poverty Curtain.* New York, Columbia University Press, 1976. [Argues that traditional development policies have failed to benefit the world's poor and advocates a "mass attack" on world poverty.]

Harding, Ann. "Transnational Capital's Future World Order and the New International Division of Labour." Paper presented at 4th National Political Economy Conference, Sydney, August 1979. [Examines the future world order—"a renovated international system (as opposed to the new international economic order demanded by the Third World)"—desired by transnational corporations through the writings of the Rockefeller-funded Trilateral Commission.]

Harry, Ralph. "The Law of the Sea and Antarctica." Department of Political Science, University of Tasmania, Hobart, 1979. [Argues that Australia is "fully entitled to sovereign rights in the Australian Antarctic Territory" and urges that the Antarctic Treaty partners should develop a regime for exploitation of Antarctic resources, as they have managed to keep the Antarctic "a zone of peace, an area of friendly scientific co-operation, in which the environment is being rigorously protected" for nearly 20 years.]

Herr, R.A. "Jimmy Carter and American Foreign Policy in the Pacific Islands," *Australian Outlook* 32.2 (August 1978). [Contrasts the continuing lack of interest America has in the Pacific Island states and its close militarily based involvement with its Micronesian colony.]

Ho Kwon Ping, ed. "Asia and the Multinationals," *Far Eastern Economic*

Review, 12 January 1979. [A collection of ten articles including one on technical cooperation among developing countries as an alternative to transnational corporations' dominance of technology transfer.]

——. "Birth of the Second Generation," *Far Eastern Economic Review,* 18 May 1979. [Critically examines the growth of "free trade zones," of which there are 50 in Asia, and expresses doubts about the benefits of these enclaves that provide cheap unskilled labor for transnational corporations.]

——. "Caught in the Oil Debt Trap," *Far Eastern Economic Review,* 19 October 1979. [Surveys the impact of rising oil prices upon developing Asian economies, and the prospects for OPEC aid.]

——. "The Implications of Export-Oriented Industrialisation for South East Asia." Paper presented at Conference on Trade: To Whose Advantage?, Australian National University, Canberra, 1980. [Describes the problems that may confront Asian economies with the onset of the micro-electronics revolution, and discusses some of the problems generally associated with export-led industrialization in Asia while pointing out that these do not form justification for protectionist policies in the West.]

International Confederation of Free Trade Unions. *Trade Unions and the Transnationals.* Published for the 12th World Congress of ICFTU, Madrid, 1979. [A handbook for trade unions in negotiating with transnational corporations, which contains information on international action by the United Nations, the OECD, the EEC, and the International Trade Secretariats regarding transnational corporations.]

Jacobs, Michael J. "United States Participation in International Fisheries Agreements," *Journal of Maritime Law and Commerce* 6.4 (July 1975). [Reviews the plethora of international fisheries agreements then in force ("It might be said, not entirely facetiously, that there will soon be more agreements on fish than there are fish to regulate") acceded to by the United States prior to the new Law of the Sea regime becoming widely accepted.]

Jupp, James, and Marian Sawer. "The New Hebrides: From Condominium to Independence," *Australian Outlook* 33.1 (April 1979). [A useful summary of events in the New Hebrides up until the end of 1978.]

Katz, Ronald S. "Financial Arrangements for Seabed Mining Companies: An NIEO Case Study," *Journal of World Trade Law* 13.3 (May/June 1979). [Describes historically the process of bargaining over the distribution of deep sea bed minerals, emphasising the difficulties caused by the "differing assumptions" of North and South negotiators.]

Koers, Albert W. *International Regulation of Marine Fisheries.* London, Fishing News Books, 1973. [A comprehensive survey of international conventions and commissions regarding fisheries up until 1973.]

Kojima, Kiyoshi. *Direct Foreign Investment.* London, Groom Helm, 1978. [A largely theoretical study of foreign investment in Asia, with emphasis on the difference between "Japanese-model" (trade-oriented) and "American-model" (anti-trade-oriented) foreign investment.]

Krause, Lawrence B. "The Pacific Economy in an Interdependent World," *Vital Speeches of the Day* 45.6 (January 1979). [Tersely provides an orthodox American justification for an OPTAD organized along the lines of the OECD.]

Krause, Lawrence, B., and Hugh Patrick, eds. *Minerals Resources in the Pacific.* Federal Reserve Bank of San Francisco, 1978. [Proceedings of the 9th Pacific Trade and Development Conference with papers on resource and commodity trade policies in the East Asia and Pacific region.]

Lewis, John, et al. "The Diplomacy of Resources," *Far Eastern Economic Review,* 28 September 1979. [Looks at Japan's efforts to ensure supplies of raw materials for her industry in the 1980s.]

Lim Chong Yah. "Obstacles to Economic Development in Southeast Asia and the New International Economic Order," *Asean Business Quarterly* 2.4 (21 February 1979). [Discusses the problems facing ASEAN countries in the context of the issues surrounding the NIEO, and suggests a more equitable distribution of income within developing countries, greater intraregional cooperation and greater intra-Third-World cooperation, including an "intra-Third-World across-the-board tariff cut for Third World products."]

McGregor, Andrew. "The Lomé Convention and the ACP Sugar Exporters: The Political Economy of Conflicting Policies." Paper presented to the 7th Conference of Economists, Sydney, 1978. [Examines the efficacy of the Lomé Convention with regard to sugar, and concludes that "because the (European) Community has not been able to reconcile domestic and external economic policy in implementing the sugar protocol, the Lomé Convention must inevitably fall well short of its purported objectives."]

May, Robert C. "Fisheries" in South Pacific Agricultural Survey, *Pacific Island Choices: Rural Limits and Opportunities.* Report to the Asian Development Bank, Manila, 1979. [Assesses the significance and potential of fisheries to Pacific DMCs of the ADB, and discusses related aid requirements.]

Mining Annual Review. London, Mining Journal Ltd., 1978. [Surveys the international mineral resource situation.]

Mitchell, Barbara, and Lee Kimball. "Conflict over the Cold Continent," *Foreign Policy,* Summer 1979. [Examines the ambivalence of American government policy towards Antarctica over the years, and urges a moratorium on exploitation until there is a firm legal base for it.]

Morgan, Dan. *Merchants of Grain.* New York, Viking Press, 1979. [Describes the manipulation of the international grain trade by governments and transnational trading houses under U.S. Public Law 480, which "was advertised as an aid program for foreign countries, but (which) above all . . . provided assistance to American farmers and the grain trade."]

Osborne, Milton. "The Extinction of Kampuchea," *The Bulletin* (Sydney) 30 October 1979. [Urges that Australia open dialogue with Viet Nam to reduce the necessity of her relying upon the Soviet Union for moral support. Australia should help to produce a settlement that accepts Viet Nam's interest in Kampuchea but works towards the re-emergence of Kampuchea as a quasi-independent state, and a "massive and continuing international aid effort will be required." Osborne's views on Viet Nam are argued more elaborately in the less journalistic *Round Table* 276, October 1979 ("Vietnam and South-East Asia: Partner or Pariah") while his latest book, *Before Kampuchea*, Sydney, George Allen & Unwin, 1979, describes the history of events that led up to the ascension of Pol Pot.]

Pacific Basin Economic Council. "PBEC Report," Los Angeles, 1979. [Provides selected excerpts from papers and other materials on Pacific business discussed at PBEC's General Meeting.]

The Pacific Community Concept: Proposals for Further Development and Co-operation between Countries of the Pacific Basin and Reaction to Such Proposals by Pacific Basin Countries: a Select Bibliography. (Networks Study No. 14) [The area studies guide on the *Pacific Community Concept*, published as *Networks Study No. 14*, arose from a request by a government department. The compilation of the guide by National Library of Australia staff in Canberra involved both manual and computerized searches, and resulted in 159 citations from monographs and serials on the topic, including Japanese language material. The guide is to be updated on a regular basis by a Current Awareness Bulletin in a series dealing with International and Policy Studies. The first issue will be released shortly.]

Payer, Cheryl. *The Debt Trap.* Harmondsworth, Penguin, 1974. [Critically examines debt financing, the IMF, and developing nations.]

Pennant-Rea, Rupert. "Who Pays the Piper?" *The Economist* 271.7086 (23 June 1979). [Surveys foreign investment in Asia, and claims that "it is much harder to find examples of multinationals ripping off poor countries (with the connivance of rich elites) in Asia than it is in Latin America. But with rare exceptions, Asian governments have not bargained so hard as to drive foreign investors away."]

Peyman, Hugh. "Malaysia's Ambitions for Tin," *Far Eastern Economic Review,* 7 December 1979. [Describes Malaysian plans for holding some of its monetary reserves in the form of tin and the impact this may have on the balance of power between producers and consumers. Payman's

"Stability and the Tin Price," *FEER*, 29 February 1980, examines the politics of the International Tin Agreement, "regarded by producers as a model commodity agreement for others to follow."]

Pindyck, Robert S. "The Cartelization of World Commodity Markets," *American Economic Review* 69.2 (May 1979). [Discusses the possibility of cartelization of commodities by developing nations, and concludes that bauxite and uranium offer the best prospects amongst minerals, while the potential gains for agricultural commodities are as yet unquantified.]

Plant, Chris, ed. *New Hebrides: The Road to Independence*. Suva, Institute of Pacific Studies, 1977. [Readings on the rise of political parties and progress towards independence up until 1977, including articles by leaders of the major political groupings.]

Race, Jeffrey, and William S. Turley. "The Third Indochina War," *Foreign Policy* 38 (Spring 1980). [Describes the background to the recent Indo-Chinese conflict. Calls for the United States to join with ASEAN, Japan, and Australia in an effort to draw Viet Nam into the Pacific community.]

Renouf, Alan. *The Frightened Country*. Melbourne, Macmillan, 1979. [Relevant and up-to-date; no better book has been written on Australian foreign policy, despite some contestable assertions and omissions.]

Sacerdoti, G., and M. Richardson. "Moving Forward Little by Little," *Far Eastern Economic Review*, 29 December 1978. [Relations between Australia and ASEAN.]

Salmon, Malcolm, ed. *The Vietnam-China-Kampuchea Conflicts*. Working Paper No. 1, Department of Political and Social Change, Australian National University. Canberra, 1979. [Background papers on the Indochina conflict, written before the overthrow of Pol Pot.]

Short, John. "RFX Still Stalks the Corridors," *Australian Financial Review*, 18 January 1980. [Problems facing the present Australian government with regard to the pricing of minerals and energy, a theme also elucidated in Michael Gill, "Aluminium Boom 'Two-Edged'," *Age*, 7 January 1980.]

Solomon, David. "How U.S. Plotted to Save Menzies," *Age*, 11 August 1978. [Uses documents now revealed under the freedom of information legislation to describe how the text and timing of the ANZUS Treaty were planned by the U.S. and Australian governments to ensure the re-election of Menzies in 1951. Brian Toohey is using similar documents from offices in Washington D.C., the L.B. Johnson Library in Austin, Texas, and the John F. Kennedy Library in Boston, Massachusetts, to write articles at irregular intervals in 1980 in the *Australian Financial Review* and *The National Times* so as to throw further light upon Australia-U.S. relations in the 1950s and 1960s.]

Strodes, James. "An Enigma at the World Bank," *Far Eastern Economic*

Review, 16 November 1979, and "An Empty Bag for McNamara," *FEER,* 28 December 1979. [Describe recent decisions of the U.S. Congress to restrict official development assistance to the World Bank and ADB in general and Viet Nam in particular.]

Subhan, Malcolm, and Ho Kwon Ping. "The Tokyo Round Draws to an Unsatisfactory End," *Far Eastern Economic Review,* 9 February 1979. [Describes the state of play in the multilateral trade and other negotiations as of February 1979, and the apparent tendency for these to be a means whereby developed countries avoid tackling the task of reducing protectionism. More recent articles are in *FEER,* 16 November 1979; 14 December 1979; and 29 February 1980 (on UNIDO III). Robert J. Samuelson, "The Trade Game's New Rules—Will Everybody Play by Them?" *National Journal,* 21 April 1979, provides an American view of the MTN and describes likely American responses.]

Suter, K.D. "Antarctica: World Law and the Last Wilderness." Sydney, Friends of the Earth, 1979. [Argues that Australia should work for an overhaul and eventual dissolution of the Antarctic Treaty, with the ultimate aim of the preservation of Antarctica as a natural wilderness area with control rested in the United Nations.]

Thayer, Carlyle A. "Dilemmas of Development in Vietnam," *Current History* 75.442 (December 1978). [Discusses the then state of economic development in Viet Nam, the issues of technology transfer, foreign investment, and grain shortages facing the Vietnamese leaders and the implications of dim prospects for Western aid. A more recent article by Nayan Chanda ("Vietnam's Battle of the Home Front," *Far Eastern Economic Review,* 2 November 1979, paints a grimmer picture of the Vietnamese economy, particularly after the limited Chinese invasion, while Derek Davies ("Carter's Neglect, Moscow's Victory," *FEER,* 2 February 1979) describes the impact that Washington's refusal to deal with Viet Nam had on its relations with the U.S.S.R.]

"Towards Wise Use of Antarctic Krill," *Ecos,* 21 (August 1979). [Examines the possibility of exploiting krill as a major source of food.]

Weeks, W.F., and Malcolm Mellor. "The Iceberg Cometh," *Technology Review* 81.8 (August/September 1977). [Examines somewhat enthusiastically the possibility of using icebergs as a source of fresh water in arid areas.]

Wheelwright, E.L. "Transnational Corporations and the New International Division of Labour: Some Implications for Australia," Gareth Evans and John Reeves, eds., *Labor Essays 1980.* Melbourne, Drummond, 1980. [Critically examines the role of transnationals and suggests an adaptation of federal government chartering of large corporations as a preliminary means of bringing them under public ownership and democratic control.

The most recent offering from the author of *Radical Political Economy,* Sydney, ANZ, 1974 and *Capitalism, Socialism or Barbarism,* Sydney, ANZ, 1978.]

Whitlam, E.G. "The Connor Legacy." The First RFX Connor Memorial Lecture, University of Wollongong Historical Society, Wollongong, N.S.W., 1979. [Describes the resource policies of the Australian Labor Government 1972–1975.]

——. "Australia, Indonesia and Europe's Empires," *Australian Outlook* 34.1 (April 1980). [Describes how the withdrawal of the Dutch from West New Guinea, the British from North Borneo, and the Portuguese from East Timor have each time created tensions between Australia and Indonesia.]

——. "Australia, Indonesia, and Europe's Empires," *Conflict: An International Journal* 2.3 (1980).

Index